May God's Holy Spirit be upon you always

Through Dark Clouds Shines Holy Light!

Nan Heathers

ISBN 978-1-0980-3286-9 (paperback)
ISBN 978-1-0980-3287-6 (digital)

Copyright © 2020 by Nan Heathers

All rights reserved. No part of this publication may be reproduced, distributed, or transmitted in any form or by any means, including photocopying, recording, or other electronic or mechanical methods without the prior written permission of the publisher. For permission requests, solicit the publisher via the address below.

Christian Faith Publishing, Inc.
832 Park Avenue
Meadville, PA 16335
www.christianfaithpublishing.com

Printed in the United States of America

To my sweet, wonderful, children, David, Scott,
Trina and DaLasa. And to my grandchildren.
They hold *all* my love!

God bless you all!

Contents

Acknowledgments 9
Through Dark Clouds Shines Holy Light!
God's Holy Light 11
Roots 12
John G. Callicutt and Hardy Roots 16
My Great-Grandmother's Song 19
More Hardy Family Roots 20
Betsy the Cow 30
A Church 32
For All Those Born Before 1945 34
Korean War Brings Life Changes 36
Leroy Mills 41
David's Accident 44
The 1960s 48
A Poem About the '60s Cocaine 51
My Salvation 53
My Children 62
Witnessing 64
Jesus and Muslims 78
Tom and Rosemary 83
Coffeehouse in Port Angeles 86
Sequim Car Wreck 89
1972 Expo 93

Bremerton	96
Elwha Pastor	97
Our Peninsula #1	99
A Man Called Clarence	131
Battle of the Mind	132
The Peninsula	134
A Tale of Four People	136
1982 Trip: Israel, Kenya and Beyond	138
Israel	140
Greece	145
Petra, Jordan	147
Switzerland	149
Egypt and Going Home to United States of America	151
Soul Patrol	154
Mother-in-Law Anne	156
A Fallen Tree	160
Our Boat	162
Tent Fire	165
God's Word and Salvation	166
The Goal of Prayer	168
My Fashion Collection	171
Finding Christ	175
Desire of the Spirit	179
The Holy Spirit	182
A Prophetic Word	183
Paint…A Gift from God	184
Fear	186
Reflecting on Spiritual Warfare	188
My Sister Cotha	191
Freedom	194
Omar, a Muslim Man	196
Hospital Stay Due to Heart Attack	199

David's Childhood Accident Consequence 204
Medicine for Life..206
Loretta Anne, a Roommate 209
Living in God's Grace..211
A Homeless Couple..213
Heaven's Grocery Store..215
Holy Angels 216
Atonement 217
Hope...219
Refresh and Grow...221
Prayers Can't Be Answered Unless They Are Prayed.......................224
A True Friendship..225

Acknowledgments

I want to thank God for allowing me to partner with Him, with my stories, and to win souls for Him. This is His book. In every step of my life and in every story, He has been and is my helper!

Thanks to my dear and best friend Nina Fisher who has been by my side with all my dreams. Nina inspired me to keep fighting the good fight—not only for myself but for those who have not had the opportunities in life I had as a child and as a grown person.

I want to express my deepest appreciation to Jeff Douglas for editing.

Also, deep appreciation to Shirley Coker for knowing me well enough and with God's help guiding her mind and fingers, to help imprint my thoughts, words, and deeds clearly on paper, recording my life.

I am grateful for all who shaped this book through counsel and advice. I hope your hearts change the world one person at a time and follow the path God has given us.

And may it inspire you to action and to a deeper faith.

Through Dark Clouds Shines Holy Light! God's Holy Light

The skies were filled with dark gray clouds.
One Saturday in the fall of 1968, I was with my friend Judy. We had dropped LSD that morning at 9:00a.m. and were waiting to come down from "our high" enough so I could drive her home.

It was now three in the afternoon, and I was coming down from the high and functioning enough to drive her home on highway 101 East of Port Angeles. I managed to drop her off safely and headed back to go home. I noticed how dark the sky looked. A thought hit me. *There is so much darkness in this world.* As I entertained that thought, rays of sunshine suddenly shot through a small hole in the dark clouds. I could feel the warmth of the beautiful rays of sunlight that covered my car and entire body. The light beamed into the car directly on me, calling me. I was completely awed by the intense, brilliant, beam of light coming directly from heaven, flooding me. That profound experience began a completely new direction for my life!

First, however, I need to go back to my roots and childhood.

Roots

Mother's side of the family was named Callicutt. Her great-great-great grandfather was William Callicutt. He came from England with Captain John Smith in 1601. He was dropped off in the Bahamas and became the very first governor there.

When Captain John Smith came back to England, he loaded the ship with new supplies and went back to the Islands. There, in 1607, he picked up my great-great-great grandfather then headed to the "new world." In 1608, he mapped out our first colonial town in Virginia with Captain Smith. William Callicutt was a goldsmith and the first person to discover gold and silver in Virginia. Jamestown began May 14th, 1607 with 104 settlers. They began building a fort to weather the cold. More setters came and relationships began. A point to make here is that a definite relationship existed between the Callicutt and Baldwin families.

William Baldwin was born in 1721. Later he met and married Mary Callicutt. Mary was the daughter of James Callicutt of Prince Edward county in Virginia. She became my great-great grandmother. She married William in 1742 and bore him three children. Mary died in 1788. William did not pass away until 1796. The Baldwin family arrived in Colonial Virginia before 1622 when they graced the ledger with bravery and distinction. During the Indian massacre, several family members lost their lives. The Baldwin's came to Virginia on ships. A few names I recall are Tygers, Maine, Tryall, Primrose, Truelove, Leaine, and Joan. They settled on the James River at Basse's Choice and Chaplain's Choice, within the original shires of James City and the Isle of Wright.

William Baldwin left a comfortable estate to those whom he loved so dearly. The estate included twelve hundred acres apart from his private home which he identified as his manor plantation. He owned and possessed twenty-eight slaves, having them identified by name and gender. There were seven men, eight boys, ten women, and three girls. To further keep some understanding of who was who, he further identified slaves known by the same name. For example, two women went by the name of Phyllis. He would call one Black Phyllis and the other he just called Phyllis. If two males had the name of Jesse, one would be named Jesse Man and the other just called Jesse. If two boys were named Sam, he would call one Sam and the other Samuel.

He showed favoritism to two negro women, Agnes and Molly. He gave them the right to choose which of their children they would like to live with after his wife died. That was a common thing to put in wills at that time. In 1865, there were slaves staying with grandfather when they were freed after the civil war. Grandfather gave them a plot of land to live out the rest of their lives. Slaves named Bob and Harry were given nine hundred acres and a copper still. Each one that was set free loved my grandfather until his death. The descendants of these former slaves still live on the land in Mississippi today.

In the late 1800s, Grandpa Eli Callicutt and a man named Mr. John Holder each gave the same amount of acreage to establish a new town in Mississippi. This new town became Holcutt, using part of each of their last names. In the 1900s, the town was vacated and flooded when a dam and the Tennessee Tombigbee Waterway was built. However, it is still posted as Holcutt to this day.

John Holder Callicutt, born in 1796, was a large landowner and one of the original settlers of Holcutt, Mississippi. He later died in Tennessee, October 5, 1880. His remains were brought back to Holcutt and buried in the Callicutt cemetery, the first person to be buried there.

May 26, 1896, a memorial park was dedicated in memory of the town and all those who made the supreme sacrifice for the construction of the waterway. The original acres of land occupied by the Callicutt cemetery remains intact and lies within the Holcutt Memorial Park area.

I also had a grandmother named Sarah who lost her dear husband George Hanover McNutt from a heart attack. She would leave home and put pine limbs in the road.

When her son asked her why she did this, her reply was "Are you crazy? I do this so that you can find me!" She had lost her mind when she lost her beloved husband.

Once she climbed up on the very top of the courthouse in Iuka, her apron full of small rocks, and threw them at anyone who said anything about her being there! The story goes that she told her son William to go get a nice man with a sidesaddle. Only then would she come down go for a ride with him! My great grandfather asked a widower, Mr. Davis, if he would be willing to help out in this adventure. He accepted. He brought his horse Whiskers to coax her down off the roof. Even then she would not budge from her lofty perch, saying, "Do you think I'm coming down to ride with that hairy devil? Get me a man I can see and dress him up if you want me to come down." They had Mr. Davis shave and cut his hair and put on a suit. Only then did Sarah come down to ride with him. Sarah died in 1851 in Iuka, Mississippi and was buried in the Pleasant Hill Cemetery.

The Lord knows when we are lost. God stands and keeps his watchful eye on us as his living stones. He calls us to come to Him. *"He that believeth on the Son hath everlasting life; and he that believeth not on the Son shall not see life; but the wrath of God abideth on him"* (John 3:36).

Like Grandmother Sarah McNutt Callicutt who wouldn't come down from her lofty perch when everyone around her was trying to coax her down, God will try and coax us to come to Him when we are burdened and heavy laden in life. God says in His Word that He would give us rest and we can be set free from our burdens in life—if we just come to Him. God longs to help and save us from our sins. He said:

> *That which is born of the flesh is flesh and that which is born of the Spirit is spirit. For God sent not his Son into the world to condemn the world; but*

THROUGH DARK CLOUDS SHINES HOLY LIGHT!

that the world through him might be saved. He that believeth not on Him, (Jesus) is condemned already because he hath not believed in the name of the only begotten Son of God. (John 3:17–18)

John G. Callicutt and Hardy Roots

My great-grandmother, Susan Virginia (James) Callicutt married John Grinder Callicutt. She was born June 27, 1853 and was eight years old when the civil war started.

Susan was a cousin to the infamous outlaw, Jesse James. He went to see her frequently and visited her often during his hay day. Jesse turned thirty-four years old September 5, 1881. He would never see his thirty-fifth birthday. Bob Ford killed him April 3, 1882.

Susan and John had nine children—four boys and five girls. After the I.C. Railroad came through their land in 1907, John and Susan's little store grew into several stores. In his day, John was the largest land holder in Tishomingo, Mississippi.

Susan passed away September 10, 1923, and was buried beside her husband, John Grinder Callicutt, in the Holcutt cemetery.

My maternal grandfather, William Eli Callicutt, was born in 1873. He was a landowner and a farmer. Julie McNutt was born January 15, 1879. William Eli and Julie were married July 25, 1895. They had six children. One of those was my mother, Sarah Viola Callicutt. She married my daddy, Clyde Hardy, who was born April 14, 1899 in Red Bay, Alabama. My mother went by her middle name, Viola, and was from a well-off and well-known family. My daddy was a son of a preacher man and farmer.

They were from two different worlds, and her family did not like this. Daddy was a young farmer and a hard worker. He loved and enjoyed the labor of his hands. Our family always had fresh vegetables daily.

Every fall, Daddy would kill a pig and cow for our meat supply. He put the pig through a smoking process, and we had bacon and hams all year long. Daddy made the best smoked meats you could find! Mother canned the vegetables and made jams from our fruit trees. Our family shared with others that had less than we did, and Mother always set a good table with enough food for our family and anyone who stopped by.

Mother said she was done having children but once again found herself with not just a single child, but with twins. Ann and I were identical in every way including our attitudes. Daddy could not tell who was who, so he would just call the closest one to him. Mother always dressed us alike until we got into our teens. That's when we started dressing ourselves different from each other. In this way we could be identified a little better.

One time, in the fifth grade, my sister and I were in different classes. She was having a math test in her class. Mr. Starter was her teacher. I was having a history test in my class. Mrs. Hitchcock was my teacher. That day we dressed alike and switched classes so I could take her math test, and she could take my history test! Mrs. Hitchcock was my favorite teacher, and I enjoyed her teachings very much. She wrote her questions and answers on the blackboard so we could study them a week before the test. I learned more about history from her than any other teacher in grade school. It was the way she taught us that allowed it to sink in and stay with us.

The bell rang. Ann and I switched and went to each other's class room to take the tests. What I didn't know was Ann's teacher would sing with her and they would harmonize together when they had extra time in class. Her teacher often called Ann up, and they would sing in front of the class. Now I was in big trouble. I couldn't carry a tune in a bucket!! I did my best to get out of singing with him and even told him I had a cold and couldn't sing!

"Come up here anyway and we'll see," he said. As soon as I opened my mouth, he knew I wasn't Ann. He said, "Hey! You're not Ann, you're Nan!" He then gave me "the look" and didn't say any more! He raised his hand and pointed to my seat as the bell rang, but I went out of the class room on a dead run! Later I saw him in the hall, and he started giving me a hard talking to, with his finger in my face, saying, "This better never happen again, young lady!"

I knew I would never be doing that again as long as he was Ann's teacher. Sometimes we switched boyfriends we were dating for the evening. We never got caught unless we told them. We were always doing things like that and thought it was funny. It was remarkable to us that we got away with all of it! Being identical twins had a downside. If one got a spanking, we both got spanked.

Ann and I were the last of Mother and Daddy's children. Ann was born fifteen minutes before me. Mother believed she was only having one child. The doctor was at the door getting ready to leave when mother yelled for him to come back. "There's another one!" she said.

"No," he said, "that's just the after birth." He checked her anyway and said, "You're right, Mrs. Hardy, there is another one, and she's coming feet first!"

Daddy said, "If they're doubling up on us, we better quit, honey!" He then passed out across mother's legs. God's hand was on me right from the beginning of my life! Mother said the doctor put me in cold, then warm water, to help bring me to life. He worked for ten minutes before I finally cried out. Mother said she didn't want to have any more children after that. She also said every place we went, people would help hold us, and we were "full-cheeked babies."

Mom and Dad did stop having babies. However, later in life they decided to adopt a young man seventeen years of age by the name of Jimmy. He was a sweet young man that talked slow and easy. He did not know we loved him as a real-blood brother. He had such kind ways about him, never raising his voice as he talked. Mother called him her sweet son until the day he died on December 3 while he was serving in Korea.

My Great-Grandmother's Song

By Susan Virginia James

(a cousin to outlaw Jesses James)
When blooming youth all in a prime
Are counting up their length of time
When Gabriel goes proclaiming around
Awake ye nations underground
When we stand at the judgment bar
Oh, then there will be weeping there
And then many a child there will say
I never heard my parents pray.
Oh, how will parents tremble there
Who raised their children without prayer
Parents, how can you hear their cry
And blame others with their misery.
When Gabriel goes proclaiming around
Awake ye nations underground
And fight with patience to the end
And you shall wear the crown
Amen

Susan Virginia James Callicutt was a devoted woman to God and raised her family in church. She exhibited her life where the world would see her light.

More Hardy Family Roots

My daddy's side of the family were Hardy's. They migrated in 1613 from Scotland to Wales and England and then to the new world. There were four generations of Baptist preachers in his family tree. When they migrated from Scotland, many of them dropped the "Mac" from the front of their last name. This means "son of" Hardy. It's like saying, "Junior here." There was no need to be "son of" in the new world. They were the first Hardys in the new world. Daddy's name was Atlas Clyde Hardy. He was born in Red Bay, Alabama, April 14,1899. The second child born into his family of ten children, all of them growing up in the south.

Fount Lou Allen Hardy, born December 30, 1875 became pastor of a church in Mississippi. When Daddy was about fourteen years old, Grandpa's life ended abruptly. He had been hunting, was climbing through a fence, and his gun went off. He is buried in Palestine Cemetery in Paden, Mississippi.

Mother saw my daddy when they were at an all-day Brush Arbour meeting. There was singing and preaching all day long. She looked up and saw Daddy walking her way. She told her mother, "He's mine if I ever get him." She had just turned twelve that June. He began to take Mother to church where there was all day singing. Afterwards he would take her to eat at his family's home. Mother said that was at the end of June. She had been dating my dad for a year but already knew she would marry him! They made plans to meet and be married by the pastor from another church. The following year on May fifth, they were married. At that time of the year, it's really hot in the south. All the windows would be open in the churches to let any breeze cool off the inside. With the windows open, she would sit by a window at the back and sneak out to go see Daddy. They were married along the roadside of the church Daddy went to in 1918. That was about the time World War I was ending.

Mother married Daddy at age thirteen—still a child and not yet a woman. Her parents weren't there for her wedding. For more than a month, Daddy did not take mother as his wife to his bed. Daddy said Mother laid down with her clothes on the night they were married, when her mother came and took her home. They knew Mother was not a woman yet. Daddy also knew by then. Mother would run back to Daddy every time her parents would turn their backs.

The day my mother became a woman, her parents let her go to Daddy. She started her family at the age of fifteen. Her first two children died from a fever that was going around in the south—a boy and a girl. My mother gave birth to nine children in all. She also raised fourteen other children that were orphans. I remember growing up in a very large family with lots of voices, plenty of play, lots of happiness, and a whole lot of love during my childhood. Only now do I realize it was a difficult time for my family along with many others in the '30s. The whole country was going through the Great Depression when Ann and I were born. My family told Ann and I about this. Daddy was working for fifty cents a day. In those times, any amount of pay was good. However, the Depression and hard times were ending when Ann and I were born. My sisters said Dad worked his farm until dark every night and was a very hard worker.

Daddy was the gentlest of souls. He always took the side of his children whenever Mother would punish us. Mother was definitely our disciplinarian. Ann and I were too young to remember the hard times. When we were older, we were told of "days of the Great Depression." My siblings, Wylo Dean, the eldest, Margaret and Cotha, all said Daddy *always provided more than enough food during the ten years of the Depression*. My family also shared with those less fortunate than us. Before I was born, Daddy made white lightning (moonshine) to help make ends meet during the earlier part of the Depression. Mississippi was a dry state, so Daddy could have gotten into a lot of trouble making and selling illegal drink if he had ever been caught. Luckily, he managed to avoid the law. He was a great provider and did what was needed for our family. He finally gave up making and selling moonshine when Ann and I were born.

When Ann and I were young, a black lady came to clean and cook for our family. She also made sure we children were clean for bed at night and always brought her sweet baby girl when she came. I admired this little black baby so much that I went to mother and asked her to please get me one to play with. I was three years old and loved watching her play. She only wore a white diaper and had lots of tiny white bows all over her head tied at the end of small braids.

Our cook's name was Mara. She would make the most wonderful molasses cookies. We were ordered to stay out of the kitchen when she was cooking, so we stood outside by the wood box. Mara would pass the cookies to us from her side. The wood box could be opened from both inside and outside. It was hinged on the top and opened upward, like a door. We could reach in and get wood or cookies without any trouble. This way we were obeying Mother and were staying out of the kitchen! We loved the cookies and always wanted more.

When a meal was ready for the family, everyone went into the kitchen to sit down and eat at the table. We were a farming family, and Mara would set out fried green tomatoes or fresh tomatoes because we all loved them. Our stove used wood, not electricity or gas, to cook our food with, which was common in those days. Mara was our cook until we moved to Washington. Ann and I were ten years old.

Three years after we came to Washington (mid 1953), we received a letter from Mara's family telling us she had died of cancer. We enjoyed her being with us growing up, and she was a good nanny for us. The south really is a different lifestyle than the northwest. My family has been here since 1949, yet I still say words that sound like they're from the deep south, either by choice or by accent. People often ask, "Where are you from?" Now that my twin sister has moved back to the south, I'm hearing her southern drawl even more. Her husband even sounds southern, and he was raised out here!

As small girls, we would spend time with Daddy's family. His family were gentle, soft-spoken people. I loved going to their homes. Uncle Grover would water his garden every evening and would turn the water hose on us to cool us off on those hot summers. He was tall, quiet-spoken, good-looking and a gentleman like my dad. We would be outside at night counting stars, looking at the black velvet sky, watching the stars fall, and making wishes as they fell. My uncle had dark hair and a wide smile. He was married to Aunt Cleo, a natural redhead who was the post master of the Tishomingo, Mississippi Post Office.

Daddy or Uncle Grover did not become Baptist preachers like their dad or grandfather. Uncle Grover and Daddy decided to break tradition and become a farmer and businessman. Daddy broke away and became a farmer, running his own farm and managing another farm for Mr. Mayo. Dad was a hard worker, loved the earth and the smell of it, and grew cotton on his farm. He would hire the black people, a hundred or more at a time, for planting, weeding, and picking cotton when it was in season. He was a smart farmer. He planted watermelon for the workers at harvest time so they would have ripe watermelon for water hydration and food while they worked. Mother often supervised the workers while they were in the cotton fields.

I remember times I would watch Daddy work. I was three or four at the time. He would make a list of the workers for the day, numbering the tote sacks that they worked with each day. He would pay the workers for the weight of the cotton in their tote sacks. The bags were weighed at the end of two rows or from picking the cotton in the middle of two rows, at the end of the day. Each person's tote sack would be emptied, weighed, and put on the cotton wagon for the mill. When the wagon was full, it would be drawn by a tractor or horses to go to the mill. Horses were used most of the time. The tractor took gas, and it was war time.

Daddy would take us with him in the cotton wagon to the mill. Always, we would be singing at the top of our voices with him. Songs like 'She'll Be Coming 'Round the Mountain When She Comes" or "I Been Working on the Railroad." Daddy would also make up something then we would have to make up words to go with his song. Daddy sang bluegrass and the blues. I learned to sing like the black people that worked with Daddy. Every now and then, a worker would put dirt in their sacks to make it weigh more, thinking that they would get away with this, but Dad knew it every time. He would empty the sacks onto the scales to see the dirt. Often mother would go out into the fields to watch, making sure the workers were not putting dirt in their totes to make the cotton weigh more. Mother and Daddy always worked well together, even when they were first married. They stayed together for life and loved their family till death.

When Daddy paid our workers, he would meet them in our backyard at the end of the day. He would take their names for the work they did that day and pay them accordingly. Many would get paid and not return for a week. This job would take forty-five minutes to an hour. While the workers waited, they would sit on a four-foot wide by ten-foot long board made into a seat, stretched over two stumps. As time went on, the blacks would pull the board from the stumps to the ground and start making music. It would sound like "ee-fa eye-fa" and make rhythmic music sounds with their mouths while also hand-jiving. Sometimes they used spoons to enhance the music. They did "hip jiv'in" by slapping the shoulders, chest, and leg, arm, or thigh to get different musical tones. Like a kind of drum beat. Two spoons hit together made a "clickety-clack" sound that also enriched the music. With their rhythmic hand jive and spoons, they made wonderful music and would start dancing. It was called buck dancing or clogging.

Ann and I would join in with them. They said, "Do like we do." Ann and I would dance with them as long as we could, picking up the rhythms and African movements! Sometimes we danced right along, keeping up with their movements, and when the music stopped, we all stopped. I always put everything I had into it every time and loved it! Sometimes the workers would give me a penny for my dancing. I would buy penny candy and was very happy.

I became good at dancing, and as the years passed, I got even better. I still love moving and dancing like they showed me. Ann always said I was the first of us to do anything. First to ride a horse, first to ride a bike, first to learn to swim, first to drive a car, and always the first of us, every time, to do anything! That has been my life. The last born but the first to try anything! My friend, Shirley, says I've always lived life and everything I did with a passion! Looking back, I know that it's true! Even when I came to the Lord, it was full-on, immediate! Only now it is with my eyes closed, and in worship, that I dance before God.

Mother raised nine of us plus fourteen adopted children. We were a happy family but also needed disciplining at times. Mother was strict and spanked us with a paddle, switch, razor strap, or leather belt. She raised us by the old school of discipline. She never spanked us out of being mean but just to correct us. The Bible says if you love your child, you will discipline them to do right. It also says that to spare the rod will spoil the child. Mother believed in disciplining her children. No one was shown favoritism.

In our home in Mississippi, we had what was called a breezeway, a long hallway the full length of the house. The breezeway was twelve feet across and had screens at the front and back ends. We did not have electricity. Our home was heated by fire places and oil lamps for light. On one side of our house was a living room, sitting room, and a dining room with the kitchen at the far end of the house. On the other side were the bedrooms and a study room. Screens allowed the wind to come in to cool the house in the evenings. On the back side of the house at the kitchen end of the hall, Mother kept three large, hundred-gallon capacity oak barrels. The barrels were full of flour, sugar, and cornmeal for cooking.

One time, when Ann and I were three years old, Mother told us to go play with Paula, our first cousin. The three of us began to play hide-and-go-seek. The seeker would cover their eyes and count while the others would hide. Ann and I opened the flour barrel, and she hid inside. I hid in the one that held sugar. Both barrels were only half full so we fit in nicely. We had stayed hidden quite a while when Ann peed in the flour. She came out covered with flour! Because of her "accident," the flour had to be thrown away, and the oak barrel thoroughly washed and sterilized! Mother was really upset and spanked all three of us. She gave it to us really good that time, and our little bottoms hurt for quite a while afterward. We were not allowed to play inside the house again.

Spanking was used for discipline, and it did correct us. The games we played helped pass the time and were full of fun when we were all together. Those games are lost on young people today. They would rather play video games, watch television, or be on their cellphones rather than play outside with siblings or neighbors. The world is changing every day. Yet no one seems to care that a lot of the changes are for the worse. Life is short, and we can work with only one person at a time. What is going to happen to our grandchildren? They will never know of the things we did as a child. We only have one life to live and hope we do something to change the world for the better and be remembered for that. God will work all things for our good. His Word tells us He will do this for His children. I believe this because God does not lie. Believe Him. He is there.

In the summer of 1944, things were changing in the crop season. Daddy worked with the POWs to pick the cotton fields that year. We lived three miles from the German prison camp in Arkansas, so Dad did not hire black people that year. He went to the POW camp and hired German prisoners to work. Mr. Mayo owned the land and a home on the next road over that Daddy managed for him. When the German POW workers left the field clean of cotton, the guards would take them back to the prison camp. Daddy paid the government camp for the labor of the prisoners. We never saw any of them again. At the end of that season, Daddy got a truck driving job hauling goods for the government from place to place. By the fall of 1945, Daddy got an automatic cotton picker. There was no need for black workers anymore.

The war ended September 2 of 1945, and our boys were coming home by November. By the next year, I was missing dancing with the black people and their soulful songs and humming. I was no longer hearing the lonely singing in the fields. There was no need for the watermelon patches to satisfy the thirst of the field workers. Life on the farm was changing. That spring, Daddy hung a swing for us in our Magnolia tree. This tree was fifty or sixty feet tall. I remember picking big green worms from it to go fishing for crawdads. We made good use of those big Magnolia tree worms. Those worms moved like inch worms. They would pull their heads up first then push forward with their tails. We picked thousands of them off the tree over the years. This tree, taller than our house, had beautiful, huge aromatic Magnolia flowers. The leaves on that tree were so full that when you looked up, you couldn't see the sky. We spent hours swinging, picking worms, and crawdad-fishing in the creek only a little way from the house. My memories of those seasons are of the warm, easy, laid-back lifestyle of the south. We watched the black velvet sky at night, looked at the stars, and made wishes on falling stars. We watched lightning bugs fly around and gathered them up in jars. We had a wonderful life.

One of those lazy evenings, a neighbor came running over with her son. His face was bleeding really bad. His dad had beaten him badly, and his clothes had blood all over them. His mother asked Daddy if he would take him to the doctor. Dad had the only car in the neighborhood, so Daddy picked him up and took him to the doctor. I cried for a long time wondering why his daddy would beat him so brutally. We had just played ball with him before he was so badly beaten. A short time later when I asked Mother about him, she said the boy and his mother had moved away and left the dad. I learned then that life was not good for everyone and that people were not always as happy as our family was. I could not understand what caused his father to beat him so severely. It just didn't make any sense to me. Daddy watched over all his girls and would have killed for any of us. He had six girls and spent as much time as he could with us all. He so loved his children.

When I was in the first grade, we were all playing outside, and I was showing some of the girls I could dance. Some of them tried to dance the same way, but they never could get it. I didn't know my teacher was watching me from the school window. The bell rang, and we all went back to our classes. The teacher pulled me aside and asked me where I learned to dance that way. I told her I learned from the black people that worked for my daddy and had been dancing with them a very long time. She asked if I would dance for the class. "Yes" was my reply! That was good because it got us away from schoolwork. I went forward and started dancing full throttle! My heart was pounding really hard as I danced with all my might.

Just as I have done with anything I undertook in life, if I started something, I stayed with it until it was done and had beat the task. When I went for something, I put everything I had into it! God made me this way. In the Word of God, He tells us not to be lazy. Be like those who have faith and have not given up. He said we will receive what He has promised us. Even as a girl, I knew this. As a woman and mother, I worked as hard as I could. I was that way with everything I did and in any job I had.

On the farm, when everyone was still living at home, Ann and I always piled out of bed later. Mother and our sisters would be in the kitchen cooking breakfast. Always, it was biscuits and gravy with sausage, eggs, fresh cantaloupe, fresh-cut or fried green tomatoes, milk, coffee, honey, jam, and fresh butter. On Sundays, Mother would make the children pancakes with homemade syrup, but Daddy always had biscuits and gravy. Mother and Daddy taught us to work hard at what we did all our lives. Mother was a hard worker her whole life. She loved her family and worked always hard for us. Even as she rested in a chair, her hands were working with something. She drew water from our well in a bucket for her flowers. They bloomed magnificently under her nourishing care every year. She made quilts that kept us warm in the winter and made doilies to dress up our home. Wherever you looked, you could see her handiwork around our home. She carefully and tenderly rocked her babies then scrubbed the rough floors to keep them clean. In the evenings, she rubbed Daddy's tired, troubled brow. Daily she helped him till the soil and push the plow. She sang to her babies when they cried and made our home a loving, safe place to live. We can hardly comprehend today, a mother working this hard. These are the memories that come and go, only to return again, and fill my mind when I think of my mother. I know one day I will see her in heaven, and we will worship the Lord together. What joy this will be. *The Bible says we will know them, and they will know us.*

In the south, Ann and I had a dog named Spud. Spud was about two years old when my brother, Aulton (Jack), took a pack of firecrackers, tied them to Spud's tail, and lit them. Poor Spud. He ran around and around and could not get away from them. Ann and I were about five when this happened. We could not understand how our brother could be so mean and do something like that to poor Spud. To this day, I cannot forget Spud running with those firecrackers tied to his tail, never stopping until the last one blew. He then ran into Ann and my arms, shaking and trembling for a very long time. Later, I walked in on Mother. She was being quite hard on my brother and said she never, ever wanted to see him do that again!

There are only two times I recall Daddy being really upset with my brother. This time Daddy did not let him go anywhere for two weeks except to work and back. The second time, when wrestling with a friend, he was told to stop playing too close to the house. He didn't listen and ended up breaking a window out of the front door. Dad took him outside and gave him a good one. Because he was Mother's only son, she had a different way of dealing with him than with us girls. She would say, "Your dad will talk to you later." But nothing ever happened nor did Daddy ever talk to him. At least we never saw it if he did. Mother and Daddy both talked to him differently than us girls. Mother would spank the girls and let my brother off with just a talking to!

Betsy the Cow

When Ann and I were about eight years old, we had a sweet cow named Betsy. Mother and my brother would milk her twice a day, once early in the morning and again late in the afternoon. Betsy, a Jersey cow, had a sweet, pretty face and was very gentle. Ann and I would have fresh milk every day from her. Brother would milk her, and as we watched him, he would squirt milk from her udders at us, with most of it going onto our faces. We had fun letting brother milk the cow and squirt milk into our mouths.

Betsy did not like snakes, she hated them. The south is full vipers and venomous snakes. One day Mother told me to go put water in the chicken tube. My dad had cut a tire in half, and this was what we watered the chickens in. I reached down to turn the water on, and a chicken snake popped his head up! For those who don't know what a chicken snake is, they are black, push off with their tail, and will run after you or a chicken just as fast as you can run. They are not poisonous (as most of the snakes are) but run after you and are very scary. I was running to the house as fast as I could and yelling for mother at the top of my lungs!

Mother came out the back door, reaching for a hoe that was leaning against the house. Running with the hoe in her hand, high over her head, she came down hard with the hoe and cut the snake's head off. The snake's head went flying, falling in front of Mother's feet. The body flew up into the air and landed on the fence, right next to Betsy. The cow went wild! Using her front feet, she kept striking at the snake over and over. She kept it up until there was nothing left of the snake. Only then did Betsy come over to me.

Betsy and I knew she had protected me. I gave her lots of praise and hugs for that heroic act. We had Betsy until July of 1949 when we moved to Washington state. We loved that cow. Daddy sold her to the Frank family next door for two hundred dollars. Their little girl was our playmate. Years later, they came to visit us for two weeks in Washington.

We also had a rooster that was a very domesticated fowl. However, he did not like my brother! He always seemed to know when my brother, Aulton, was milking Betsy and always caused him stress. He would wait for my brother to come out of the barn, then fly at him, talons barred, trying to hurt him—something he did quite often. That rooster constantly waited for brother to finish his chores, then the rooster would fly at him like a raptorial bird, getting my brother in the back of his legs and hurting him. It became a daily thing for that rooster.

One afternoon, Aulton was coming from the barn with a full bucket of milk. Here came the rooster running full speed to attack him again! The rooster nailed my brother hard, right in the back of his legs. The bucket of milk went up over his head and came down right on top of him, getting him and his clothes all wet and sticky. Aulton was really, really mad then and yelled, "That's it! That's the *last* time you're getting me, Mr. Rooster!" The next thing we knew, brother shot that bird with Daddy's shotgun. Guess what? We had chicken and dumplings for dinner that night. And that was the end of that mean old bird! My brother had no more worries, and we enjoyed every bit of our delicious chicken dinner!

A Church

When my brother was around fourteen, Aulton and two friends of his went to the far end of Dad's cotton fields. There was an old, large, house not being used that Daddy had closed up. One of the black men came to Daddy and asked if they could use it as a church. This man said he was their preacher, and Daddy said yes! Every night the noise from their singing and preaching would fill the night stillness, bringing their music to our ears. We loved it, and in the south, they can really sing. The black preacher would preach the same thing every night, with the same stories. He always said, "If Gabriel should blow his horn, *are you ready? Say amen!*" He would repeat that over and over again, with everyone shouting, "Amen!"

My brother and his friends, hiding in the rafters, were being very still and very careful so they would not be seen nor heard. The preacher was closing his sermon the same way as he did every day. He would call for everyone to say "Amen" and ask, "Are you ready for Gabriel to blow his horn?" This time, just as they were all worked up, Lynn took his horn and blew it. The people in the building hit the door as fast as they could! Everybody was running over each other trying to get out the door!

The preacher ran with them, but his jacket got hung up on a nail on one of the homemade benches. As he was trying to get free of his jacket, he kept shouting, "I'm not ready! I'm not ready, Gabriel! I'm not ready!" Fighting furiously, he finally broke free from the nail holding him back and ran out the door! After the preacher was gone, my brother and his friends came down from the rafters and ran out the building. Aulton came home and told Mother and Dad about it.

He was laughing the whole time telling them his story. Daddy did not think it was funny and told Aulton that what they did was not right, they were being prejudice, and things like that would rot their very soul!

"Things like that" are very dangerous to our faith. It will ultimately take hold of us and the way we think. I know this because I saw a lot of that in the south. The courthouse in the town I was born had signs that said: "Blacks Only" on one end and the other end "Whites Only." These signs were also on water fountains that were for all to drink from. Those kind of principles in our lives will come out if we are around that behavior too long. Our standard for righteousness should arise to outrage. Where is our moral compass? This world is a degenerating, cutting place, and we are watching it go downhill fast. It is in trouble racially, politically, economically, and spiritually. We watch this on the daily news. We are a broken nation and society. Our only hope is in God and with Christians around the world praying. God is the only one to heal our brokenhearted nation. Thank God we have prayer back in the white house. That gives our nation hope once again.

Christians should be an encouragement to all people we talk to every day. Luke 10:2 tells us *"The harvest is great but the workers are few. Pray ye therefore that the Lord of the harvest that he would send forth laborers into the vineyard."* (This is people that are without God that he wants us to talk to for their salvation.) Our restless searching world needs answers and the gospel of our Lord Jesus Christ IS the answer. He is our total need.

For All Those Born Before 1945

(From the Internet)

We are survivors! Consider the changes we have witnessed: We were born before television, before penicillin, before polio shots, frozen foods, Xerox, plastic, contact lenses, Frisbees, and the pill. We were born before radar, credit cards, split atoms, laser beams, ballpoint pens, before pantyhose, dishwashers, clothes dryers, electric blankets, air conditioners, drip dry clothes, and before man walked on the moon. We got married first, then lived together. How quaint can you be? In our time, closets were for clothes, not for "coming out of," bunnies were small rabbits, and rabbits were not Volkswagens. Designer jeans were scheming girls named Jean or Jeanne, and having a meaningful relationship meant getting along with our cousins. We thought fast food was what you ate during Lent, and outer space was the back of the Riviera Theater. We were before house-husbands, gay rights, computer dating, dual careers, and computer marriages. We were before day-care centers, group therapy, and nursing homes. We never heard of FM radio, tape decks, electric typewriters, artificial hearts, word processors, personal PCs, yogurt, cellphones, and guys wearing earrings. For us, time sharing meant togetherness—not computers nor condominiums. A "chip" meant a small piece of wood. Hardware meant hardware like hammers, nails, and building materials. Software was not even a word! In 1940, "Made in Japan" meant it was a piece of junk. The term *making out* referred to how you did on your exam. Pizzas, McDonald's, and instant coffee were unheard of. We hit the scene when there were five and ten-cent stores, where you could buy things for a nickel or a dime. For one nickel, you could choose to ride the street car, make a phone call, or buy a Pepsi. Stamps to mail one letter cost only three cents. Postcards were only a penny each. You could buy a Chevy Coupe for $500. Who could afford one? Gas was eleven cents a gallon, and that was a lot of money back then. In our day, cigarette smoking was fashionable. Grass was mowed, Coke was a cold drink, and pot was something that you cooked in. Rock music was a grandma's lullaby in a rocking chair! Aids were helpers in the principal's office. We were certainly not before the sexes were discovered, but we were surely *before* sex change and transgenders! We made do with what we had when we were born. We were the last generation that was so dumb as to think we needed a husband to have a baby! No wonder everyone is so confused and that there is a generation gap today! *The gap is so wide.* I'm looking to heaven where there is no gap.

Korean War Brings Life Changes

In 1949, my brother Aulton, nicknamed Jack, joined the army. He was stationed in Fort Lewis, in the state of Washington, on the outskirts of Olympia. We also had two older sisters who were married by this time, and they were also living in Washington. My sisters kept talking to my parents over and over again until they convinced Mother and Daddy that they should see my brother Aulton off before he was to be shipped out to fight against North Korea. Mother and Daddy packed up what they wanted and could use. We loaded the family onto a train in Little Rock, Arkansas headed to Tacoma, Washington. This train trip took four days. My sister had acquired a huge Victorian house for us which had lots of rooms in it. The house was in Olympia, Washington area. The house was painted white, and we lived in it over a year. It was the funniest thing. Our family left our home in Little Rock, Arkansas, a big city, and ended up in a tiny town called Little Rock near Olympia.

Every weekend we lived there, my brother Aulton would bring three or four fellow soldiers home with him for the weekend. Sometimes it was a different group of young men each time when they visited. The soldiers would come in late Friday night, around 9:00 or 10:00p.m., so by the time they arrived, we would be asleep. Ann and I would rise early Saturday morning, and soldiers would be sleeping on the couch, chairs, and floor in the living room. Many times, my brother and the soldiers would cook meals of bacon, eggs, biscuits, and gravy or whatever they could find to cook in our kitchen. Mother had gotten close to one of them. His name was Jimmy. This soldier had no family. He had grown up living wherever he could find a bed. Mother loved him, and he became our brother, even taking our last name. He never knew what his last name was.

Jimmy Hardy was one of the youngest soldiers. He was only seventeen when he joined the army. He was a fair-headed, blond boy who was an orphan. He came to Washington from the south. Like most southerners, he was a nice, easygoing young man. Our entire family loved Jimmy from the start, but Mother truly loved him like her own son. She adopted him before he went to Korea. Mother went to Olympia and filed papers to do this. He really was our brother by law then. If I remember right, Mother told me she paid twenty-two dollars to file the papers before he went to Korea to become a true Hardy and used this as his last name. My sister Margaret had told Mother how to file the papers.

Bobby Wyatt was another soldier. He and my sister Arminta fell in love during one of the weekends the soldiers visited my parents' home, just before he went to Korea. Bobby married my sister at seventeen years of age, on March 6, 1950 in Olympia, Washington. Bobby and Arminta didn't get to go on a honeymoon before he was shipped out to Korea. Arminta was seven years older than Ann and me. I was the youngest born fifteen minutes after my identical twin sister Ann. We were the last of mother's children to be born at home. Jimmy Hardy died in Korea. He was brutally killed there, according to a newspaper article entitled "Story of a Korean Death," told by the brother of GI Aulton (Jack) Hardy. It happened as follows:

The story of the brutal killing of his brother by communist troops and of being trapped for 120 hours by the enemy has been revealed by Corporal Aulton C. Hardy, twenty to his mother who resides on Route 4 here. Aulton's brother Jimmy was killed December 3 in Korea, He was one of the American soldiers found shot in the head with his hands tied behind his back. Corporal Hardy wrote to his mother Mrs. A.C. Hardy that Jimmy had volunteered to go on a patrol mission in place of his brother-in-law, who hadn't had any sleep for four days. The two brothers Jimmy, Aulton, and their brother-in-law, Sergeant Bobby Wyatt, were together in the same outfit in the Second Division. No one sent out on this patrol for which Jimmy Hardy volunteered had returned. It was some time later that Aulton and his brother-in-law, who were still together, were trapped by the enemy. It was during the retreat from Northern Korea after the Chinese Reds had entered the Korean War.

Bobby Wyatt and Aulton C. Hardy both returned to the states from Korea. Aulton's service in Korea earned him a Purple Heart, a commendation medal, and three good conduct medals. He died February 16, 2005 in Warden, Washington. Bobby had an extensive military career, and by the time he retired he had been in Korea, Germany and had served two terms in Vietnam. Bobby was awarded five good conduct medals and also received one army commendation medal.

He was married for many years to my sister Arminta until she died in 1983. Within a few months, Bobby followed her in death.

In 1951, my family moved to a place called Midway on the old Hwy 99. Daddy and Mother bought a restaurant there which they called Midway Café because it was midway between Seattle and Tacoma. It had a checkerboard décor with black-and-white checkerboard floors with the counter tops, tables, booths, and bar stool seats all red. Across from the restaurant, on the other side of Highway 99 was a large dance hall called the Spanish Castle. This was a place where big bands would come to play music with band singers. My sister Cotha and my siblings would go there and listen to the big bands and to dance. My twin Ann and I were eleven years old when we learned how to dance ballroom style. However, Mother would only allow us to go out on weekends until 11:00p.m. If we were not home by then, we would get it and not allowed to go the next weekend. We were always careful to be home on time so we would not get into trouble. We were eleven to fourteen years old. Those were some of the best days of our lives.

The '50s were good times at our home. Our doors were never locked, not even when we went to bed at night. The nation was a much safer place then. I remember those days with great happiness and realize what a clean, nice time we had growing up.

I had two sisters that never had any desire to learn how to dance nor to go out at night. They also married at a very young age. They were both married a long time. One was married sixty-five years before she died and the other was married fifty-eight years before she died. Both were very good cooks and would make seven to eight apple pies at a time and share them with the whole family. We were a close family for as long as everyone was alive.

Daddy bought a green 1949 Chevrolet coupe for my brother, Aulton, so he would have a car when he got back to Washington State from Korea. My brother, Aulton, took his coupe to Moses Lake. Later he went to work for the government in the State of Washington as a top agricultural executive. He would tell the farmers which crops to plant, such as potatoes, corn, or other crops. The government bought him a plane he flew from job to job to save traveling time. They also purchased him a new pickup every year. He loved his job up to the day he died. Aulton married Evelyn, the singing sweetheart of Moses lake. She was well known in eastern Washington, singing on the local radio stations in the area. Aulton joined her singing the lead with Evelyn. He married Evy (that was her nickname). He also had a long career with the agriculture department. They had three daughters—Sandy, Julie and Wendy. Aulton and Evelyn were married over fifty years. He died in 2002. My daddy's last name of Hardy died with him as there are no more boys to carry on the name.

My parents were married fifty-seven years. Mother was thirteen, and Daddy was nineteen when they married in May of 1918. World War I was just ending. In the south, many people married young and started their family. My parents had never kissed anyone else romantically before they met. Mother was Dad's first and only love. Daddy always lived like a good Baptist son. In all my life, I never heard him swear or use any profane words. Dad's bad word was John Brown, using this as a swear word when something went wrong. My parents were very happy together. They loved each other until they died. I can't ever remember Daddy raising his voice to Mother, but she would yell at him sometimes! He was very gentle, and his word was the gospel truth. Daddy died of lung cancer in 1975. Mother followed him more than ten years later with stomach cancer in 1986. The Bible says to be absent from the body is to be present with the Lord. I believe both of my parents are in heaven with the Lord! With this knowledge, I feel comfort knowing I will see my parents again when I die. The Bible says that *we will be known as we are known,* meaning we will recognize each other in heaven, so I will know my mother, Daddy, and my family. What joy and happiness lives in my heart that we will see our loved ones again! Praise God! We will see them again because we believe in Jesus Christ. He is the way that we come to God in repentance according to John 3. Jesus said, "I am the Way, the Truth, and the Life and no man comes to the Father but by me." We will go there knowing this before we die. For me to think about all of this, is happiness in my heart. From all my siblings, only my twin sister, Ann and I, are alive today. She lives far away and I have not been able to see her for years. My sweet family lives here on the beautiful Olympic Peninsula with me.

The Bible tells us that everyone that says "Lord, Lord" is not going to heaven. In other words, there are people that know about God and that he is real but have never asked God to forgive them their sins and asked Him to come into their hearts. God tells us in John 3 we must be born again in him to see heaven. He will give us a new way of life in Him, when we are born again in Him.

Leroy Mills

In the summer of 1955, I was fifteen years old and had just completed junior high school. I wanted to get a job, so I lied about my age and said I was eighteen years old. I went to work at a cannery in Olympia. Break time for everyone came, and a man came up and started to talk to me. He said his name was Leroy Mills. He had been working there when the cannery opened for the fruit canning. The bell went off and break time was over and we both went back to work. At noon, the lunch time break came, and here he was again, a handsome tall young man with dark hair and steel gray eyes smiling, coming over to me once more. We started talking again, and he asked me to go out with him Friday night for a movie. I told him I had a twin sister who worked on the other side of the cannery. He said he had a friend he would bring along so we could make it a double date. This was the start of our dating. I didn't know it yet, but I had just met my future husband. He would become the father of my three beautiful children—David, Trina, and Terry Scott. I married him at the age of sixteen. We were married for eight years. I didn't know at the time he would never be faithful to our marriage nor the abuse I was about to endure.

My husband Leroy, the children's dad, had been working out of town as an iron worker and coming home only for weekends. I did not know it yet, but my husband was planning to kill me. He had taken a million-dollar life insurance policy out on me! His plan was to take me scuba diving, deep in the water, pull my breathing hose from me, and hold me underwater until I drowned.

My husband's best friend, Mike Neely, also a scuba diver, often dived with my husband. In the summer of 1963, Mike had been going out with my older sister for almost a year. However, he was keeping it from my husband Leroy, even though they were best of friends on and off the job. We decided to plan a trip to Tillamook, Oregon to dive and camp out in tents. Mother had agreed to babysit the children, so I was happy to go with them. Having no worries, I was looking forward to diving and the beauty of being in the water.

I was standing alone on the beach when Mike came up and asked if he could talk with me. I said sure and asked, "What's up?"

He began this way. "If something were to happen to you while you were scuba diving, what would happen to your children?" He then said, "I am going to tell you something, but you have to promise me not to say or tell anybody what I am going to tell you."

By then I was having some anxiety but said, "Okay, I won't tell a soul."

"Your husband has taken out an insurance policy on you, and I believe something might happen to you. I don't want you to dive alone with him ever!"

I pledged I would never say anything about it. The picture was clear what he was saying! I realized he wanted to say more but wouldn't. That evening I looked out of the tent and saw Mike standing on the beach looking at the water where Leroy was diving. I walked out to check on things and to talk a while with Mike. Leroy had gone diving to get us some crab for dinner. Mike told me then my husband was going to kill me for the insurance and said for me to be careful.

At an earlier time, Leroy had revealed to Mike what he was planning to do. Mike was worried about all of it and watched over me carefully that weekend. In just one day, my life totally turned around, and I didn't know what to do. I started to remember Leroy cleaning his guns and the two times they had gone off in the house. The first time I was in the living room ironing the children's clothes. The gun went off hitting the ironing board, ricocheting up, and going through my blouse from one side to the other without touching my skin! The second "accident" happened when I was standing at the bathroom sink washing my hands. Fortunately he missed again. I dismissed them as accidents at the time because that's what he said they were. However, after the conversation with Mike, I now knew they were not accidents like he said they were. I knew Mike was right. The picture was very clear; I had to leave him very soon to keep from being killed.

I talked with my sister Margaret about what to do. She had a sixty-five-foot trailer home she and her husband would give to me for the children and myself to live in. That would be my way out. We made arrangements to move my trailer close to Kent. Later we moved it next to my mother in Port Angeles. I was never going to worry about Leroy again. It wasn't but a short time later that my phone rang. I was told my husband had fallen from three stories, was badly hurt, and would not get any better—he would never recover. Before that, I was always watching and wondering if Leroy might come in the night to do something to hurt us. There were so many times odd things had happened, and I wondered if Leroy had his hands in it. Now that I look back on this, I realized that, yes, he most likely did. I would never have to be afraid of him trying to kill me again. I knew this was God's way of protecting me and my children. He did give me three wonderful and beautiful children from our marriage.

Leroy died a sad and lonely man in Portland, Oregon and had no one when he died. Only a half-sister came to see him as he lay dying in his bed. Leroy did have three other half-brothers and a stepmother, but he didn't have anything to do with them. He always had tales about his stepmother. His relatives all lived in Salem, Oregon and could have seen him every day, however, none of his family didn't seem to care about him at all. I did love him at one time. He was the father of my children, and I wanted them to see him one time before he died. I prayed for him, hoping he would get better and have a better outlook on life, but he died in his bed alone.

David's Accident

David was born in August of 1957. When he was three years old, in the late summer of 1960. My daughter, Trina, was eighteen months old, was born April of 1959. My youngest baby, a son, Terry Scott, born in April of 1960, four months old. We were living in Golden Dale, Washington. My husband Leroy Mills was a steel construction worker and worked on the John Day Dam.

I had gone to Portland, Oregon for the day and left the three children at home with my sister Cotha babysitting. It was a Thursday morning when I got home from Portland.

When I arrived home around 10:30a.m., I found out my three year old son, David, had been playing with a ball in the front yard. Around 9:00a.m. in the morning, the ball had rolled into the street. My three year old had chased it right into the path of an oncoming car! David was hit by the car and thrown "sixty" feet into the air. Higher than the fifty-foot tall tree in the front yard of our home. The ambulance had been called immediately. Paramedics had packed my unconscious David into the ambulance and drove him to Yakima.

I had already left Portland and was driving toward home when the accident occurred. This was before cellphones, so there was not any way to communicate with me while I was traveling. As soon as I arrived home, a policeman who was present informed me of the accident and was ready to drive me to the Yakima Hospital immediately. A neighbor who lived next door offered to babysit the other two children, so my sister Cotha and I left with the policeman.

Yakima, a bigger city, was about two hours away from home. It took several hours for the policeman to drive us to Yakima. I began praying aloud for the first time in my life on that ride. I was extremely distraught as I did not know the Lord but knew my firstborn son was seriously injured, and I did not want him to die. During that trip between home and the hospital, I made promises to God I do not even remember as I was pleading with Him to spare the life of my son. It seemed like an extremely long trip.

When we arrived in Yakima, it was about 12:30p.m. The medical staff said they did not know the full extent of David's injuries yet as he was still unconscious, and his head was packed in ice to keep the swelling down. They then took me into the ICU room where David was. When I saw his almost lifeless, unconscious body lying there, I almost fainted. It broke my heart! I remembered Daddy told me many times that God answers prayers. "Oh God, my son is only three years old, and he is almost dead." I even thought he might be dead already because he looked so bad. Instantly I began to pray again, "Oh, God," and gently placed my hand on David's little belly and prayed with a desperate feeling in my heart. I stayed that way for hours.

My sister Cotha contacted our parents to let them know about David. It was a five-and-a-half hour drive from Kent, Washington where they lived, to here, in Eastern Washington. Someone had gone to the John Day Dam to inform Leroy his son had been hit by a car and was in the hospital. Leroy left his job and drove to the hospital in Yakima. He arrived early that afternoon and stayed with me most of that night. He knew I had a support system of family and friends who would be there for me. Friday morning, Leroy got up early after a few short cat naps during the night. He then drove three and a half hours to his job to work all day.

In the meantime, my parents arrived in the mid-afternoon. Daddy came and stood in the doorway of the ICU and spoke to David. "How is my grandson? Do you want a popsicle?" Miraculously, David opened his eyes for the first time since the accident and said, "Grandpa!" I was so thrilled when I heard his little voice! Oh, the happiness inside! The elation of hearing him! I was so happy! It was the first sign of hope that David would live! He looked at Grandpa and said weakly, "My belly hurts, Grandpa." The nurse told us he did not know it was his head and not his belly that hurt so much. Actually, everything probably hurt in his little body after flying sixty feet into the air, coming down and landing on hard ground! That was when I recognized God's hand in it. God *had* heard our prayers, and He had touched my little boy!

After working all day Friday, Leroy freshened up then came right back to the hospital and stayed all weekend with me. Mom and Daddy got a hotel room near the hospital for the first weekend. I was able to go there and sleep for a few hours while my parents stayed with my son. On Monday, they returned home to Kent, all the while praying for their grandson. David's head injuries were extensive, and the bones of his head were cracked all around even down into the bridge of his nose. The only thing holding his skull in place was his scalp. Daily I saw David getting a little better. The doctors were doing something right. At first they were taking him for x-rays, measuring his head, putting in a drain tube to help with the swelling. It was something different every day. When the swelling was finally down, they scheduled surgery to put a metal plate in his head. This was to help him stay alive.

I stayed at the hospital the whole time David was there. Leroy went to work all week and returned to the hospital weekends. My sisters Cotha and Margaret watched our younger children, Trina and Scott. Mother also watched them about eight days during that time. David continued improving every day and even sat up at times. After the swelling went down sufficiently, about twenty-two days, the doctors did surgery. Putting a metal plate in his head gave him room for growth because he was so young. They had to drain fluid out through his ear. For a while, the medical staff would not allow David to get out of bed at all. Quite challenging for a three year old to only lay still in bed! After more recovery, they put a helmet on his head before they would allow him to get up. From that time on, he once again started improving daily. David had to wear that helmet for a full year.

After the surgery, the medical staff was doing something different to improve my son's condition. They did physical therapy daily to improve my son's condition, making sure he could walk, always stressing the importance of him wearing the helmet every single time he was out of bed. He also had speech therapy, making sure he could talk and communicate. God answers prayers—I was seeing evidence of this every day. Leroy was with us at the hospital weekends and others came also. My parents, my husband's parents, friends, and family all worked out a schedule of who could help and be with me. One would sit with David while I napped in the sleeping area of the hospital. Other times while someone else was there that had rented a hotel room, I had the luxury of being able to go to their hotel and really sleep awhile. This went on over three weeks, then I was able to take my son home!

God, the doctors and nurses saved my son's life! What *joy*! I knew my sweet son was going to live, and I also knew God had answered my prayerful cries.

The 1960s

I *would like to paint you a picture of the 1960s.*
It was an era like none ever before it! While war was raging in Vietnam, the hippy movement in America was in full swing! Wild music, psychedelic drugs, drugs, and "coming out" homosexuality was suddenly "in." On TV, award shows, football games, and everywhere else you could think of, "streaking" (running naked) was seen. Music festivals were suddenly the place to be. Woodstock, along with hundreds of smaller musical and drug-infested festivals, ruled. The killing of both Kennedys, John and Robert, numbed the country as did the senseless murder of Martin Luther King. There seemed to be no limit, restriction, or boundaries what anyone did or tried to do. The "mantra" of the '60s was "Do what feels good." Most horrific was Charles Manson, along with his cult of female followers, who brutally murdered Sharon Tate (pregnant at the time) and others in her home. Charismatic religious group movements of love and goodwill to others abounded. Hippies handed out flowers as an act of love and charity, a "gift" for public benevolent purposes. It seemed like it was everywhere in America (but it wasn't). People were saying, "Make love, not war" and "Turn on and tune out!" The hippy, free love movement exploded in San Francisco and rippled out from there. Haight Ashbury, San Francisco, and California were the places to be!

The joy-filled, happy, loving and carefree 1950s were behind us. A brand new era of the 1960s crashed onto the scene with a bang! Touting free love, drugs, LSD, and wild, psychedelic lights and music! It was also a year of political and social turmoil in the United

States and Europe. Here in the States, in 1968, Robert F. Kennedy was running for president. This forty-two-year-old senator from New York was the brother of President John F. Kennedy who had been shot in 1963. The new Kennedy campaign headquarters were at the Ambassador Hotel. June 6, 1968, as Robert walked through the hotel after his speech to the nation, he was shot. He was rushed to the Good Samaritan Hospital but died. His wife Ethel was by his side. It was another sad day for America.

None of us alive today knows when we're going to die. Life on earth is short. The Bible says it is a vapor of smoke going up and gone. We all hope to live our lives in fulfillment; we are all brothers and countrymen together in life. God wants us to live in peace and love, making Him, Christ Jesus, the center of our lives. Sharing with others during our short time on earth, with the purpose of becoming Christlike in our hearts.

In the early 1960s, a psychologist experimenting in psychedelic drugs was Timothy Leary. Leary, highly educated, was conducting drug experiments. Those experiments were within the law until they became unlawful in the late 1960s. He was arrested often enough to see thirty-six different prisons worldwide. Many people took LSD on sugar cubes or what was called Blue Dots. Timothy popularized the catchphrase that promoted his philosophy: "Tune in, turn on, drop out!" Leary married Barbara Plum, adopted her son Zachary, and raised him as his own. He also had several godchildren, including actress Winona Ryder's daughter with Archivist Michael Herewith. By the 1980s, his colorful lifestyle made him a desirable guest at the A-list Hollywood parties. Leary's daughter, at age forty-two, was arrested in Los Angeles for firing a bullet into her boyfriend's head as he slept. Twice she was ruled mentally unfit to stand trial. While in jail, she tied her shoelaces around her neck and hung herself. From 1989, Leary began to establish his connection to conventional religion. However, his life was still full of people he had talked into taking LSD and his philosophy of turn on, tune in, and drop out.

The Vietnam War was on the news every day. News reported a US soldier was killed there every six minutes! More than 58,000 American servicemen died in Vietnam. That pained my mind. I was young, in my early twenties and believed I would live forever, giving God no thought. Leary's easy sayings had a lot of people wanting to know more about LSD. LSD, Cocaine, Pot (Mary Jane), and every drug you could think of became popular and seemingly easy to get overnight.

A Poem About the '60s Cocaine

In the 1960s, there were a lot of drugs going around, and the following poem (circa 1960) is credited to *Larry Jackson* and was dedicated to Maureen and her recent recovery.

>Beware my friend. My name is cocaine, Coke for short.
>I entered this country without a passport.
>Ever since then, I've been hunted
>And sought by junkies, pushers, and plain clothes dicks,
>Mostly by users who need a quick fix.
>I'm more valued than diamonds and gold;
>Use me just once and you too will be sold.
>I'll make a schoolboy forget his books,
>I'll make a beauty queen neglect her looks.
>I'll take a renowned speaker and make him a bore;
>I'll take your mama and make her my whore.
>I'll make a schoolteacher forget how to teach;
>I'll make a preacher not want to preach.
>All kinds of people have fallen under my wing;
>Just look around and see the results of my sting.
>"I've got daughters turning on their mothers;
>I've got sisters robbing their brothers.
>I've got burglars robbing the Lord's House.
>I've got husbands pimping their spouse.

I am the King of Crime, and the Prince of Destruction.
I'll cause the organs of your body to malfunction.
I'll cause your babies to be born hooked.
I'll turn the most honest of men into crooks.
I'll make you rob and steal and kill.
When you're under my power, you will have no will.
Remember, my friend, my name is Big "C".
I've destroyed actors, politicians, and sports Heros.
I decrease bank accounts from millions to zero.
Well, now you know, what will you do?
Remember, my friend, it's all up to you.
If you jump in my saddle you'd better ride well.
For the white horse of Cocaine
Takes you straight into hell!

(This poem left me totally awe stricken. I lived the "hell," and I cried as I read this prolific commentary. Send this poem to everyone you know whether or not they are addicted. It's the message that needs to be spread throughout the world. The message that needs to be taken into every heart and mind. Praise the Lord for your poem, Larry, and God bless you. You gave us hope to go on.)

The person who wrote the poem, Cocaine, knew what he was writing about. It will *take you to hell and rob you of all you have.* We use our choice to go where our mind takes us. The battle of good and evil goes on in our mind. *We will always have a choice between good and evil.* God is always there, waiting to come into our hearts. He will also make a way when we follow His will. We need to learn about the glory of Christ. Jesus bore my suffering and pain at the Cross. He gave His life so we might have everlasting life. This is for all of us.

(My interjection: "For we wrestle not against flesh and blood, but against principalities, against powers, against the rulers of the darkness of this world, against spiritual wickedness in high places" [Ephesians 6:12, KJV].)

My Salvation

One October Saturday, in the fall of 1968, the skies were filled with dark, angry, gray clouds. I lived in Port Angeles, Washington at the time and a friend, Judy, lived twenty miles East of Port Angeles, toward Sequim.

Judy had spent the night. We "dropped LSD" that morning at 9:00a.m. and were waiting to "come down" enough so I would be able to drive her home. Around three in the afternoon, I was finally down enough to function and decided I was okay to drive. We headed east on Highway 101. I managed to drop Judy off safely then headed back West. I noticed how gray and dark the sky really was when a thought hit me. *There is so much darkness in the world.* As I entertained this thought, the sun suddenly shot through a hole in the clouds. Beautiful, bright rays of sunlight beamed down to the earth! I felt like it was calling me directly. It literally filled my car with brilliant, blinding, pure Light! Hitting directly on my lap, I was completely in awe of the incredible rays of this pure light shining right down from heaven above, directly on me! Only seconds earlier, the clouds had been very dark and angry! This was absolutely amazing! It filled me with wonder.

The trip on LSD today had been a spiritual experience like God was dealing with my head. Thoughts of God continued going through my mind for several day after that particular LSD trip. I went home and told my husband about the trip and about the religious thoughts I was having. Dave Lundgren, my second husband, was a musician. Jack Belmont was his band's booking agent. Jack had booked their group to play in several places over the next few months and also arranged for me to go with David. It meant going to four other states for six weeks then come home. However, as it turned out, I had to stay home with my three young children instead. The band was preparing to leave and start the tour in a few days but wanted some marijuana to take with them. I made arrangements to go to Seattle on Saturday afternoon to get a brick of marijuana. I went by bus (120 miles one way) to Seattle and purchased the marijuana for them to take on tour.

While there, I decided to spend the night with my friend, Patti Dana, and her husband Jim. They lived on Capitol Hill in Seattle. I would return to Port Angeles by bus the following day, in the afternoon. Around mid-morning, we had scrambled eggs for breakfast. Before I was to leave, Patti suggested we smoke a joint. We sat in a circle on the floor, lit up a joint, and started passing it around. When it came to me, I took the joint between my finger and started to take a toke. *Immediately* I heard God say, "*Today is the day of your salvation!*" I did not understand what was going on in my head, so I got up from the floor and passed the joint to the next person without smoking any. I went to the bathroom to wash my face. I pulled my false eyelashes off, laid them on the sink, and looked at my reflection in the mirror. The thought *What is salvation?* came rushing through my head along with other thoughts. Confused and not knowing what was going on, I went back into the living room and asked Patti and Jim if they knew what salvation was. We were all sinners in the habit of dancing, using drugs, and drinking alcohol every night! In addition, I was a cocktail waitress, bartender, and a go-go dancer in the same club. *None of us knew anything about salvation.*

I thought, *If that was you God, then show me where you want me to go and what you want me to do.* My grandpa was a Baptist preacher, but salvation was a mystery to me even though I had prayed when David, my son, had been hurt. *And just a week ago, I had seen that Holy Light shine through the dark clouds into my car!* So I challenged God: *Okay God, what is the right church that you want me to go to? There are so many churches that claim to be the right church, so show me, and I will go.*

On Sunday, I went to the bus station with those thoughts still running through my mind. I took the early afternoon Greyhound bus home from Seattle to Port Angeles. I didn't realize it at the time, but God's hand was already hard at work to get my life headed down the right road!

At that same time, in Port Angeles, a man named Everett was working on the wiring of a neighbor's house across the street from my mother's home. Everett took a lunch break. As he did so, he noticed Mother's beautiful flower garden. He went across the street to take a closer look at the flowers and began talking with Mother, who was outside. After admiring her flowers, he told mother about a southern gospel group called The Gaithers that was going to sing that night. The event would be at the Assemblies of God church, pastored by Frank and Jean Cole. Mother must have told him about me and her concerns about the direction my life was going in as she gave Everett my phone number. He wrote it on his brown paper bag lunch sack before he went back across the street to finish his work for the day. Then he went home.

The Greyhound bus arrived in Port Angeles around 3:00p.m., and Dave, my husband, picked me up at the bus station. We drove home, and I gave him the kilo of marijuana. He took the suitcase, evenly divided the marijuana for all four band members, then left to give each one their share of the weed. I stayed at home when he left, and by four-thirty that afternoon I was cooking dinner.

A short while after Everett arrived home from work, he asked his wife Julie, *"Where's my paper lunch sack?"* As usual, Julie had wadded the lunch sack up and thrown it into the fireplace to burn. A fire was going, but it had not burned up the paper sack! It had rolled off to one side! (More God in action!) Everett retrieved the sack from the fireplace and called me at the number mother had given him.

I was cooking dinner when the phone rang, and I answered. A man's voice said, *"My name is Everett and my wife's name is Julie. You don't know us, but we would like to invite you to come to our church tonight."* Instantly, I knew God was answering my challenge from noon today! (The "Okay, God, which church do you want to go to?" question!) Here is a man I've never met, inviting me by phone to the Assembly of God Church! This must be where God wants me to go! I accepted the telephone invitation to go to his church that night.

Everett asked if he and his wife needed to come pick me up for a ride, but I said, "*No, I will meet you there.*" God's hand was already at work!

My husband came home about 5:30p.m., and we had supper together. I left the house at 6:15p.m. and went to the church that evening looking like the sinner I was. I wore a very short, shiny silver mini-skirt. It was one of my go-go dancer outfits, but short mini-skirts had just come into fashion! Yes, it showed I was definitely a worldly woman and a sinner!

As I entered the church door, a man with a big smile approached me and introduced himself. Of course it was Everett! Next, he led me halfway down the church auditorium and introduced me to his wife, Julie. She had me sit next to her. The Gaithers began singing real southern gospel music! My tears started to flow. I cried through the whole music service. Literally through the whole thing! Finally, they invited anyone who wanted to come to the altar and accept Jesus to come forward. I believe I was the first one out of my seat! They led a closing prayer, but I stayed at the alter and cried and prayed for about ten minutes before Pastor Cole came down and talked to me. He read Romans 10:9–10 then asked if I believed Jesus died for my sins and that the Bible is the Word of God. "*Yes!*" was my answer. Next Pastor Cole led me in the sinner's prayer. I already cried so much, my false eyelashes had fallen off and my make-up was badly smeared, washed off by the multitude of tears, yet I was ecstatically happy!

Mrs. Cole, the pastor's wife, gave me a copy of Modern News for Man. This is the Bible version in English, easier to understand than the King James Version which was first published in 1611. Modern News uses a style of words we speak in America rather than the common King James version. Mrs. Cole told me to read this "Modern News for Man Bible" book as much as I could at home. Immediately I had a great desire and insatiable hunger to do that because I truly wanted to learn more. I just had an experience which changed my life and eternal destination forever! I knew, quite literally, I would never be the same as when I entered the church earlier that evening! I began to read my new Bible right then and there. I wanted to soak in as much about my new faith as I could and quickly! In between people in the church coming up to me, I was already looking at and reading the Bible Mrs. Cole had given me.

I left the church and lit up a cigarette as soon as I got to the sidewalk. As I did, I heard the Lord speak to my heart. He said, *"Is not this what I delivered you from?"* Right away, I quickly flipped that cigarette as far away into the road as I could. It was the very last time I ever lit or smoked a cigarette. God *completely* delivered me from cigarettes and *all* things of the world, like alcohol and drugs I had held so dear just the night before. *I was now a born again person in Christ.* Like Jesus said in St. John 3: *"Unless you be born again you cannot see the kingdom of heaven."*

Going home from church that evening, my mind was twirling with the words I heard the preacher say earlier. By flipping that cigarette into the road, I *knew* God had spoken directly to me. What was I going to tell my husband? How was I going to explain the great excitement I felt within me? In my heart I prayed, *Oh God, help me please to be what you want me to be!"* I knew something about what was happening in my heart and mind. I had been to church as a child but had never asked Jesus into my heart for real. Even when my son, David, had that bad childhood accident, my family and I had prayed to God, and my son was healed, I still had not accepted and served the Lord. I continued to live my own way, partying, dancing, drinking alcohol, and using drugs. No one had led me to salvation before this night. A true conversion experience. I accepted Jesus personally in my heart.

As I drove home from church, my mind was on all the things I heard and experienced that night, but soon realized I was home. I pulled into the driveway and my thoughts went instantly to my husband. I began to dread what I "knew" was going to happen as soon as I told him what occurred to me at church. I got out of the car. As I was walking into the house, I looked up and said, "Hi."

Dave was standing in the doorway. He looked at me as I walked in and said, *"What's up? What happened to you? Your face is shining!"* Wow! There was a difference in me that was clearly visible! Praise God! I knew I felt different. There was a new energy I felt inside like a weight had been lifted off my shoulders. It was a clean, sweet happiness! I felt real joy inside for the first time in a long time, and I was at peace deep inside my head.

I told my husband the news of my salvation. He heard me, but it had absolutely no meaning for him. It went over his head because he did not know anything about salvation. His mother brought him up Catholic, and they did not go often to church. His daddy was a sheriff, his mother an RN, and both worked all the time. They completely lived a worldly lifestyle, the same as me before this night. They went out drinking and dancing. His dad was also a member of the Masons. Their lifestyle was not Christ-like. His parents were in their late forties. Dave and I married when we were in our twenties.

My husband started talking to me about the tour his band, Dick Fisher's Trio, was going on. They were booked for five places. Las Vegas, Nevada; Billings, Montana; Alaska; back to Seattle; and then home for a two weeks tour stop. That night, Dave and I talked for a while. I told him I could not go with him on the tour because it would cost me my salvation. He was definitely not impressed! He said, *"Well, if you don't go with me, I'll find someone who will."* After my husband left to go on that tour, he only came home twice. The first night of the tour in Billings, Montana, where his band played, he met a girl named Linda who went with him. A few weeks later, I found out I was soon to have Dave's baby.

One final note about Dave is this: my husband came home one last time that fall after his band's tour started. I was glad to see him, however, I had found out he was already having another affair, so I told him we were not getting back together. He filed divorce papers quickly. A few weeks after he left us, the divorce was finalized. He did not know I had conceived a baby on his visit home and never knew I was having his baby until after we divorced and he had a new wife. I felt so lonely after my divorce. In August, I had a sweet baby girl, and I named her DaLasa.

Dave's heart stopped on him in the early 1980s. He was still playing in the band, using drugs, drinking, and partying until he died. The saddest thing of all was he never asked God into his life and never accepted Jesus. Dave saw the light of the Lord's presence in me the night I was saved, but he chose to walk away from our family.

He could have chosen to respond to that light, but he did not. He is not in heaven. He is separated from God. He has no redemption. Eternal pain and torment are his. There is no longer any hope of salvation for him. His soul will live forever with no joy or love—only in hell. Jesus said in His Word that His Spirit would not always deal with man. Now Dave was gone.

That is why we need to share our faith and tell other people about Jesus. He has a plan of salvation and a better life and a great eternal home in heaven for each person who invites Jesus into their hearts. What is your choice? Eternal life and great blessings by accepting Jesus? Or torment and pain by doing your sinful deeds in this life? Just being a good person means we are following flesh. The devil is the enemy of mankind and the enemy of God. Even the good people who try to live right need to accept Jesus. We have all sinned and fallen short of God's glory and God's standards. Each person has a choice to make. Jesus will not force us to accept Him. If you choose Him, then heaven will be your eternal home, if you refuse, you will be separated from God for all eternity (forever). I started going to the Assembly of God church every time the doors opened. Then I started going to the Pentecostal Church, the Four Square church—really any church that had an event going on. I was very hungry for God. I was studying and reading the Bible a lot, trying to gain as much knowledge about my new salvation as I could. I was praying for hours every day and reading the Bible. Just two weeks after getting saved, God gave me His gift of His Holy Spirit, with the speaking in other tongues. That was a wonderful thing that happened to me. I felt so much of God's love, there are no words to tell you about this. *His love is so great*! My mind was only wanting to praise Him and talk to Him for hours on end!

The first person I led to the Lord was Patty Ward. Let me tell you about Patty. She was already dating my husband and sleeping with him without my knowledge. After my husband left on the tour, a friend told me Patty and my husband had been dating. When I learned this, I went over to Patty's house, knocked on her door, and confronted her directly! She told me "No," denying dating my husband. I knew she was lying, without a doubt, but I left and went home.

A few days later, the phone rang at home. We had a three-day snow fall. but the sun was finally out today. Vicky, a beautiful redhead that looked like a movie star, called and asked if I could come over to her house. Snow had fallen off her roof that night and made her afraid Jesus had come to take all Christians away. She called to see if I was still here and to ask me to come over. She was afraid that God had left her behind. (She was speaking of the rapture).

I went over to her house, knocked on the door, and went in. Vicky was babysitting Patty's son, Aaron, who was about two years old. I asked Vicky why she was babysitting Patty's son, and she said Patty was on a logging run with my husband! He drove a logging truck when he wasn't playing music. This trip took about ninety minutes going to Forks and back. When Patty returned to pick up her child, I confronted her about the sin of fornication. Patty thought I meant her husband Frank was cheating on her, but he was not, even though they were separated. I confronted Patty about her relationship with my husband, David. I believe Patty's relationship with my husband started at a multi-band musical get-together in September of 1967.

After Patty got saved, we became close Christian friends. We had true forgiveness. This blew a few minds around town, seeing us together as friends. Eventually Patty and Frank got back together. They stayed married until both went on to be with the Lord.

Patty and I opened a coffeehouse together in her basement for young people. They could come talk to us or the pastor about issues. It became a place to help them stay off of drugs. We got our pastor and a few other people to come help with it on weekends. We did bring people to the Lord. Later in my life, many of the young people that got saved there have told me they're still standing for Jesus. Tom was one of them. He was fifteen years old when he was coming for coffee and blessings! Tom later became a preacher and stayed in Port Angeles. He fed the homeless, and people accepted Jesus through Tom. I read once that 85 percent of what you hear and see, your mind retains. I think about all the young people we talked to about the Lord and wonder how many are still standing for Jesus today or how many minds retained what was said.

THROUGH DARK CLOUDS SHINES HOLY LIGHT!

Our eyes see so much every day in our lives. What a wonder it is just to see. A human eye has one million nerve fibers in each optic nerve and all are connected to the brain. We can figure out things like the distance to any object we are looking at just by seeing it. Isn't that a wonder? God created our eyes and that ability! He made all of us. He gave us life by putting His breath in us when He made Adam. What a wonderful God He is! God gave us this beautiful world we live in. But because of the fall of man through Adam and Eve's sin, there is human sin all around us. Our sinful heart can pull us away from God. Even when we are young or old, our sinful nature separates us from God. We need to find Jesus and ask Him to come into our heart to overcome sin and to be reconciled to God. After we accept Jesus into our heart, we need to grow in our faith by doing things like reading the Bible, going to church, and fellowshipping with other people who are following the Lord.

My Children

All three of my children accepted Christ as their Savior while they were still children. My son, Terry Scott, was ten years old when he was filled with the Holy Ghost in my living room while praying in the evening. He received the evidence of speaking in tongues.

Trina was eleven years old. She was going up the steps to her room. She heard my friend Patty Ward and I praying in tongues. Trina said to God, "*I don't know if I believe in this tongue talking, but if it is of You, God, I want it.*" As she reached the top of the stairs, she lay down on the landing and received the gift. She spoke in tongues! A Chinese-sounding language and spoke over thirty minutes. A vision started. She said she saw a big mountain blow up! It was a vision of the Mount Saint Helens volcano that blew May 18, 1980. Other things she saw and described are still taking place in the world.

One night I went to bed at the usual time of 10:00p.m. I heard God call me. He said, "*Arise, arise.*" Twice. The house was quiet. It was in the still of the night. I listened but heard nothing else, so I lay back down. About two minutes later, I heard it again, "*Arise, arise.*" I got up then and started to put my clothes on. The Lord spoke again. This time I recognized His voice. He said, "*Arise, arise, and preach the gospel to every creature.*"

Then I argued with God and said, "*But God, how can I go when I don't even know the scriptures?*"

He said, "*Go, trust Me with all of your heart, and I will direct your path.*" I did not even know this was scriptural, but I found it the very next day in my devotional Bible reading. Mark 16, the Great Commission, tells us to go into all the world and preach the gospel. That became the confirmation scripture of my calling. Proverbs 3:5–6 says, *"Trust in the Lord with all thine heart; and lean not unto thine own understanding, and He will direct your path."*

After a good night's rest, I got up and started preparing to move to Seattle. That was in the fall of 1968. I didn't know the whys or the wheres, but I knew I had to go when God calls!

That afternoon, I sat the children down and told them I was divorced, and I felt like God was calling me to move to Seattle. My mother was still alive and well, living in Port Angeles. She would watch my kids much of the time, but the children were old enough to watch themselves. When I moved to Seattle, at night I would get a sitter to stay with them.

I started praying, *Lord, if you want me to go, then I must rent out my house in Port Angeles to someone I can trust*. Early that afternoon, I had started supper when my friend Patty Ward came over. She was the very first soul I had led to the Lord here in Port Angeles. She stated she and Frank needed a place to live, did I know of a house they could rent? Of course! There were my renters! Within a week, I was happily on my way to a new life in Seattle.

From the children's dad, Leroy (critically injured in a fall), we had received an insurance payout. Also, the children each received social security benefits on his behalf every month. Those monies allowed me to pay all living expenses! I just rented out my house in Port Angeles and that would, in turn, pay for a rental house in Seattle.

When I began to pray to the Lord, "Lord, if you want me to go, then I must rent out my house in Port Angeles to someone I can trust," He answered *immediately*. The next evening, friends Patty and Frank stopped by and wanted to know if I knew of any place they could rent! God is good! All the time!

In the pages to come I pray you will truly understand what I am saying and that it takes root in your hearts. I'm praying there will be many souls added to heaven because you have received this into your souls. I am saying it over and over in many different ways.

Witnessing

Hal Bredison, a preacher and the one who led Pat Boone to the Baptism of the Holy Spirit, had a church in Victoria, Canada (Victoria is eighteen miles across the Strait of Juan de Fuca from Port Angeles). Our group of believers would get on the Black Ball ferry in Port Angeles to Victoria and go visit his church. He was a good brother in the faith with a love for the lost. Hal told me about a lady named Linda Meisner who was working for the Lord and preaching in Seattle.

At the end of November, I went to Seattle to hear Linda preach. She was preaching about her time in New York City, participating and leading "The Girls to God" program to set them free from drugs and sin. She was good at what she did, and now she was living in Seattle. Linda started the Jesus People movement there. I had been saved for five or six weeks at the most. After I heard her preach, I came home to Port Angeles carrying a new spiritual fire within me! I wanted to see people meet Jesus and get saved. My friends thought I had taken too much LSD and had flipped out! This was because I was boldly telling people about Jesus, and people were getting saved all around me! I was bringing in five or six new people into the church every single week!

As the Lord had told me, I moved. I arrived in Seattle. I had trusted God and rented a big house with three bedrooms upstairs and a large basement. I knew God had called me, so I acted on His Word. My twin sister Ann was already living close to Seattle, so she helped me find this house in the university area. I got in touch with Linda Meisner of the book, *The Cross and the Switchblade*. She was Deb in the book, and now she was here, leading the Jesus People

Army in Seattle. She started this work of the Lord. I found out Linda was to preach in a local church that night. She and Trina MacDougal were already working around the University of Washington, bringing souls to the Lord. It was wonderful how God was using these ladies.

I went to hear Linda preach in Seattle that night. After the church service, I told her I had just moved to Seattle and that God had called me to work with the Jesus People Army. Linda and her friend, Trina, welcomed me with open arms. I began to work with them right away. We went to her house that very night and began to memorize scriptures that would lead people to faith and trust in Jesus as Lord. We used the Romans Road to Salvation verses:

A) "For all have sinned and fallen short of the glory of God" Romans 3:23.
B) "The eyes of your understanding be enlightened" (Ephesians 1:18).
C) "For by grace are ye saved through faith; and not of yourselves: *it is the gift of God*" (Ephesians 2:8).
D) "For the wages of sin is death; but the gift of God is eternal life through Jesus Christ our Lord" (Romans 6:23).
E) "But God commendeth His love toward us, in that while we were yet sinners, Christ died for us" (Romans 5:8).
F) "For by grace are ye saved through faith; and that not of yourselves: it is the gift of God: Not of works lest any man should boast" (Ephesians 2:8–9).
G) "That if thou shalt confess with thy mouth the Lord Jesus, and shalt believe in thine heart that God hath raised Him from the dead, thou shalt be saved. For with the heart man believeth unto righteousness; and with the mouth confession is made unto salvation" (Romans 10:9–10).

Every night the Jesus People Army got together. My children went with me. I also had them in school in Seattle by November. We had good neighbors, and my kids would come home from school and watch TV or do homework, then they went with me in the afternoons and evenings.

Linda began to talk about opening a coffeehouse and asked if we wanted to volunteer to help run it. Of course we did! Her vision was to offer free coffee and donuts to anybody who would come into the coffeehouse. We would witness to people who would come in to enjoy the free coffee and donuts. Linda found a place four doors down from the penny arcade on Madison to establish this coffeehouse.

Linda had a band playing Christian music, and on the wall coming in you would see Bible verses from John 3:1–8. Many people would ask us, "What is being born again? What does it mean?" The door would be open for us to tell them about Jesus Christ. What joy it was to see so many people come to believe in Christ! Night after night, the Jesus People would lead people to the Lord. We grew so fast that Linda had to find a large house to start teaching the Word to the men. Soon, I had ten ladies staying at my home. We had to build twin beds from two-by-fours for them to sleep on in the basement. Nightly we would pray and study the Bible. There was much happiness and love. You could feel God's power in us, and we couldn't wait for the next evening so we could be together again. Prayer kept us going. Sometimes hours would go by. We would look at the clock and realize we had just prayed three hours or more! I cannot adequately describe to you the sweet joy and feeling God would give us.

When we were witnessing to each person we talked to, we would say, *"Jesus loves you! Do you know that Jesus Christ died for you?"* As we talked to people and taught the Word of God, each person would say "yes" as the Spirit of God moved. The truth of what we were saying would become a light to their hearts as they said yes to receive Jesus. We watched God's hand moving every day and lives being changed. There is nothing on earth that is better than being a part of His work. This makes your faith climb, and you learn to trust God with everything in you.

I was also seeing people around me get delivered from demons and people getting filled with the Holy Spirit every day. It was not just one or two people but many! Oh, the gladness and love that came with this! There was nothing else on earth that could give us so much happiness and joy!

We would stop everyone and tell them about the saving grace of Christ. And of course we would tell them about the Holy Spirit if they had been saved right there on the streets! Often they would get filled with God's Holy Spirit. Other people would stop and check out what we were doing. Then some of those who were watching who would also get saved! We would go through the scripture verses again. Sharing these verses always gave us another soul for God. We told each person who got saved to memorize Bible verses to help them stand strong every day. *"But grow in grace, and in the knowledge of your Lord and Savior Jesus Christ"* (2 Peter 3:18). For God has given us all a will and each person has that choice to receive salvation. God does not force anyone to be saved. He gives us a free will. The devil has put lies and deception in our minds, and we will follow that deceiver if we do not ask Christ to come into our hearts. So using their own free will, they are choosing the burdens of life and have rejected all invitations to have God in their life. We must preach the gospel for people to know the truth.

God doesn't want anyone to go to hell. He died for all of us. He wants us to be set free and to get saved. We look at the Word of God to find some of the righteous people God used. In Exodus 4:10, Moses was a righteous man called by God to lead His people out of Egypt. God told him to speak to the people on His behalf. Moses said, "I can't because I have a speech impediment." God wants us to speak up and lead other people to Him. We're the ones God wants to use to bring others to belief in Christ Jesus. Whenever you feel empty, start telling someone about Jesus. God will give you a fullness and a refreshing of his presence when you do. Sharing the gospel is the start of caring about others. When you know Christ, no matter how dark a moment in life seems, we always have hope and love. Ninety-five percent of Christian nations have never led anyone to Christ. Isn't that sad? When so many people are dying and going to hell, Christians will not or do not speak up with Gods salvation message. God has called *all* of His Children to do so. God doesn't want anyone to go to hell. He died for all of us. He wants us to be set free and to get saved.

Jonah didn't want to go to Nineveh when God told him to go to preach to them. God was going to judge the people of Nineveh because they were doing many evil things. However, the Ninevites were Jonah's enemies, yet God wanted them to have an opportunity to repent. Since Jonah did not want to go preach to his enemies, he got on a ship going toward Tarshish, a different direction and away from Nineveh. He did not want to obey and do what he knew God said for him to do. A great storm came upon the ship. The sailors were fearful because the ship was about to sink. This storm was fierce. They were all praying to the best of their ability when they discovered that Jonah was running away from what God had told him to do. Then they became more afraid. It was decided Jonah had to be thrown overboard, so the ship could be saved. As soon as Jonah was off of the ship, that storm from God stopped instantly! These sailors came to faith in Jonah's predicament. When Jonah landed in the water, a big fish came up and swallowed him. After three days in the belly of the fish, Jonah came to his senses, repented, and confessed he had sinned by going away from Nineveh in disobedience to what God told him to do. He prayed for God to help him. God then caused the big fish to spit Jonah out on the beach, very close to Nineveh.

We are much like Jonah in a lot of our ways. We do not like to get out of our comfort zone to take a stand for the Lord. But God has called each believer, all of us who know Jesus Christ, to preach the calling of the Great Commission. To tell all people He came so that *all* can receive salvation. He wants all Christians to serve Him and to do what He has told us to do. Jesus died on the cross and rose again for that very reason. God does not merely want us to be a quiet example, although He can use that quiet witness and our good deeds also. Do we invite our friends and people we meet to meet Jesus and invite them to church? We should! God truly wants us to boldly tell others of the gospel. Sometimes we are the only light the world ever sees. By our actions and good choices, witnessing the Word, people around us see Jesus and hear about him. We need to be the salt on the earth for Him. What does this mean? We are carrying the "salt" as a seasoning with the flavor of Jesus in everything we do. However, we're much like Jonah in a lot of ways. We do not like to get out of our comfort zone to take a stand for the Lord. In hell, there is no hope and no love whatsoever. A person who goes there after their body dies will never get out! Never! Their body is dead. However, our soul is eternal. Our soul will never die. The soul of a person who does not accept Jesus will be lost in torment forever! *Forever*! We can't even imagine how horrible the torment, pain, fire, and demons all around us will be in terrible darkness.

If you have not received Jesus in this life, hell waits for you. We use our free will to choose the place where we go.

Remember, the battle is in our minds, when we pray for Christ to come in. "Resist the devil and he will flee from you" (James 4:7). We will always have spiritual warfare in this life. When we come to accept Jesus Christ, our minds will go in a direction that has a desire to serve Christ or our flesh. We have to kick out the junk of this world we have accumulated during our life's journey. Read the Bible, think on God's Word, meditate on it, truly ponder its meaning so that you can win the fight. God loves us *all* and wants us to meet Jesus and follow Him as we go through life and as we make decisions. It is all in our minds.

As I worked on the streets with the Jesus People Army, what happened every day was this: we saw lost people coming to know the Lord. My life was so full and so blessed. Christ was the center of the very witnessing we were doing as individuals and as a team.

Linda said we were going to set up a booth in the Seattle Kingdome and witness there. The Battle of the Bands was playing that weekend. The whole Jesus People Army would be there to take a stand for the Lord!

One girl who stopped in had a lot of issues, yet Christ was doing a work in her life. She was on LSD and was very high. Staying with her was a difficult task because her mind was going places hard for us to follow. Praise the Lord, someone suggested we take her to the Halfway house we set up. People were present there who had dealt with this before. We learned later she had been saved and gave her heart to Jesus. Oh, what great joy!

Over the weekend, we had paper files that told us three hundred people had given their hearts to Christ during the Battle of the Band event. We rejoiced for a week after that! It was such a joy in our hearts to know we had led that many people to faith in Our Lord! God rewarded our work for Him in a way beyond anything any of us had expected or believed possible. This was outside the scope of ordinary experience. We were seeing God's hand at work every day. This is something we miss in everyday life if we do not look to God.

As we continued to work for Jesus on the streets, our faith was soaring! Only God could give this to us! One Friday night, we were all at the coffeehouse. A young man named Edward was saved and filled with Holy Spirit that night. He had gone to the men's house to stay the night with the other Christian men. Linda had set up this house for men that were saved to help them grow. We would have Bible study early in the afternoon before witnessing.

One Saturday night, Edith and I went down by the Penny Arcade. A black man was standing outside the door. He was pimping four women to support a $500 habit a day. He stood there about an hour and talked to us. As we began to pray for him, one of his ladies came up. Now we had two people praying that we were leading to God! We were so happy! The man's name was Ken. The woman's name was Joyce. Ken went to the men's house that night, knowing he was going to go through withdrawals from drugs.

The next night, Ken was in trouble with extreme withdrawal pains. Edward, the young man that had been saved the week before, went to the men's house, saw Ken, and said, *"Why are you not stopping this?"* He took Ken by the hand, sat him down, and *commanded* the pain to stop, in Jesus' name! It stopped and Ken was filled with the Holy Spirit!! His withdrawal symptoms stopped instantly! Ken later went to Bible school, became a Pentecostal preacher, and is preaching in Seattle—even today.

I often think of Ken sending up prayers for all who came to God in the '60s and '70s. We have forgotten names over time, but God knows. When we're old, we consider things of the past with hope for the ones God touched as they passed through our lives. I still rejoice when I think what the Lord has done for the ones around us today. The Lord is always present, waiting for us to come to know Him in His fullness. Revelations 3:20 tells us that Jesus stands at the door of our heart and knocks. Will you let Him come in? Prayer is the world's greatest wireless connection. And often we pray, not thinking God will hear us. He Hears! Remember, His Word says, *"If we have faith of a mustard seed"* (Luke 13:19), which is very tiny, we are able to tell that mountain to be removed, and it will go away! See Mark 11:23.

We were seeing this every night as we worked for God on the streets of Seattle. One night it was getting quite late. We didn't like being on the streets too late after dark. I had parked my car behind the coffeehouse and restaurant, on a side street by the UW (University of Washington). As Edith and I headed toward the car, we looked up and saw eight or nine shady-looking men in leather clothes nearby. It spooked us, and we did not want to walk past them. Edith started praying, and I loudly said, "In the name of Jesus!"

That group of men parted like the Red Sea, and we walked right through their midst to my car! We sat in the car and rejoiced as we went to the girl's house that night! "Thank You, God!" was our praise! We saw God's hand time and time again as we happily went out witnessing for Jesus. Letting our light shine and the contentment we felt was pure joy! Our experience with God was full. Our prayers to God were as much as we could pray in a day in the Spirit! Often, we spent hours in prayer in the Spirit!

In the Book of Acts 1:8, it says:

> But ye shall receive power after that the Holy Ghost is come upon you: and ye shall be witnesses unto me both in Jerusalem, and in all of Judea, and in Samaria, and to the uttermost part of the earth.

This means to everyone we talk to, starting at home. They can receive the Holy Spirit after they ask Jesus Christ to come in and forgive their sins. God's Word is the seed. We are to take His Word and plant it in others *by telling them the good news of salvation*. People will respond as they hear. God commissioned us to preach the gospel, when He saved us. We need to put action to our words and pray as we sow, by planting the seed of His Word into people's lives. This is why so many people responded to our actions in the '60s and '70s. The Jesus People Movement was strong because we prayed and went out to others and planted seeds of God's Word.

We did not get embarrassed nor did we have shame. God would help us choose the right words as we went out and as we spoke. God would bring people to us then give us the words we needed in our minds. Just praying in your closet will not get the job done. We have to put action to words. Prayer does not cause others to be born again. Prayer will help and moves God's hand, but we have to share the gospel and speak it. We reach souls by sharing the gospel. Remember, freedom is found by being bold. Jesus said in John 14:12, *"Verily, verily I say unto you, he that believeth on me, the works that I do shall he do also; and greater works than these shall he do; because I go unto my Father."* Jesus wants us to reach the lost so they are saved by taking His Word to the world. It is not enough to just sit in church and learn all you can. You must take the Word you have learned to the people who need salvation. Prayer and action by witnessing causes God's hand to move and lives to be changed. How will people get saved if we do not preach the news of salvation?

God said in Luke 8:16, *"No man, when he hath lighted a candle, covereth it with a vessel or putteth it under a bed; but setteth it on a candlestick, that they which enter in may see the light."* This is for all of us who know the salvation of Jesus Christ. Also, Mark 16:15 says, "Go ye into all the world, and preach the gospel to every creature." We must take this to heart and be God's laborers and live His Word.

God is not a man that changes his mind. He means everything He said in His Word. If we sit all the time in church and never lead anyone to Christ, what will we say to Him when we stand in front of Him? We can't say, "But Lord…" This just will not get it. I can just see Christ crying because He will have to judge each one of us.

He that saith I know Him (Jesus) and keepeth not His commandments is a liar. (1 John 2:4)

THROUGH DARK CLOUDS SHINES HOLY LIGHT!

The word which ye hear is not mine, but my father's which sent me. (John 14:24)

Let us reason together. We as Christians need to sow the seeds of the Word of God. When others hear the Word, they will open their hearts to the truth and receive Him. God moves on His people to win souls, but yet many will not sow His Word. He has commanded us to sow in Mark 16:15, and yet we still sit in church not saying anything to others to win them to Christ. The real strength of the church is the preaching of the gospel and the fellowship that we have with other believers. I read once that only 5 percent of believers will bring someone to the Lord. That leaves 95 percent that do not bring anyone to the Lord. My heart hurts when I think of this. So many people are dying without Christ. As Christians, we need to do something to change our nation by telling others about the gospel. *"For I am not ashamed of the gospel of Christ: for it is the power of God unto salvation to everyone that believeth; to the Jew first, and also to the Greek (Gentile)"* (Romans 1:16).

Jesus said in John 3:3, *"Except a man be born again, he cannot see the Kingdom of God."* We have to be born again before we can see the kingdom of heaven. Without hearing the Word of God, we can't be born again. As Christians, we all need to be powerful witnesses for our Lord Jesus Christ. As we witness to others,

> *But the Comforter which is the Holy Ghost, whom the Father will send in my name, He will teach you all things and bring all things to your remembrance. "Whatsoever I have said unto you."* (John 14:26)

He always gave us the Word in our minds when we were witnessing. God is faithful to do all that which He said He would do. Study the Word of God and when you need it, God will bring it to your remembrance as this verse states.

People die, and when they leave this world, there is no coming back. Your soul will either go to be with God or to Hell. We all have a choice.

> *If thou shalt confess with thy mouth the Lord Jesus, and shalt believe in thine heart that God hath raised Him from the dead, thou shalt be saved. For with the heart man believeth unto righteousness; and with the mouth confession is made unto salvation.* (Romans 10:9–10)

Christ said, "*I am the door: by Me if any man enter in, he shall be saved, and shall go in and out, and find pasture*" (John 10:9). When Christ spoke on the cross He said: *"Father, into thy hands I commend my spirit"* (Luke 23:46). Then He died for all of us. Now we have to use our own free will to come to him and serve him. Or we can go into the world and let our "flesh" (sinful ways) take over. Jesus said in John 8:24,

> *I said therefore unto you, that ye shall die in your sins; for if ye believe not that I am He, ye shall die in your sins.*

> *He must increase, but I must decrease.* (John 3:30)

When we come to Christ with an open heart, He will honor this. You start praising Him until the worship comes, then keep worshiping until the answer comes.

He will fill you with His Holy Spirit. Christ told the people in Jerusalem to "[w]ait for the promise of the Father, which saith He, ye have heard of me. For John truly baptized with water, but ye shall be baptized with the Holy Ghost not many days hence" (Acts 1:4–5). Then, in Acts 2, He came as "a sound from Heaven as of a rushing might wind, and it filled all in the house where they were sitting."

> *And there appeared unto them cloven tongues like as of fire, and it sat upon each of them.* And they

were all filled with the Holy Ghost, and began to speak with other tongues, as the Spirit gave them utterance. (Acts 2:3–4)

This promise is unto you and to your children, and to all that are afar off, even as many as the Lord our God shall call. (v39)

It is a gift for every one of God's children. We again have a choice to ask God for all that He has for us or to be content with a wishy-washy, mediocre life. We are not born a winner or a loser, we choose.

God's covenants demand action on our part. He does not make covenants with double minded people. He wants people who will trust Him, obey Him, and engage with Him on a daily basis. He doesn't want puppets that just wait for Him to pull our strings before we will move. He wants thinking, feeling, caring, and passionate people to respond willingly to Him. He wants us to take action. We serve a God of passion. He is a God of action!

We are what we think. It is in our hearts! God wants to be in our heart and in the way we think. God is the Word. "Think the Word." Every day we need to read the Bible and apply the Word to our mind and thoughts. We need to be led by God's Holy Spirit and not by our fleshly hearts and sinful ways. If we follow our own impulses and emotions, we would be lost and kept busy with worldly things. For those who want to live on a higher plane and to be led by God's Spirit, the Lord always goes before us. He is able to keep us, if our mind stays on Him. Don't worry about others or what they think of you. Don't let worries get the best of you. Remember, Moses started out as a basket case (haha)! God is with us. He has appointed our pathway and knows all of our needs. He also knows what is best for each one of us. Praise God for all things and this will inspire your soul. The greatest triumph that can come to my soul is to rejoice in the Lord always. This will help to build your faith and defeat the devil. God is in. We are what we think. He is in our hearts. God wants us to be aware of Him in our heart and in the way we think. God is the Word. *"Think the Word.*" Every day we need to read the Bible and apply the Word to our mind and thoughts. We need to be led by God.

We can pray, doubt, and do without. Or we can pray, believe, and receive from the Lord!

The Lord hears our little, short prayers, and even when we think, He knows what it is. God hears prayer even when we just think it. God is Good. He will not withhold good from His children. Whenever I stand in need, I know He is present. "He said, *'Come unto Me, all ye that labour and are heavy laden, and I will give you rest'*" (Matthew 11:28). God wants us to think about Him in all that we do. He will take care of our needs and troubles.

Let your mind dwell on God and His Word. Fill your mind with scripture verses and the power of God's Word. This will establish your heart. Remember, a day of worry is more exhausting than a day of work. Satan always paints a dark picture in our mind. Satan is a liar. Try prayer and praise instead. God will bless you for it. Anxiety will leave. Do not be anxious about anything, *"but in everything by prayer and supplication and with thanksgiving, let your requests be made known unto God. And the peace of God which passes all understanding shall keep your hearts and minds through Christ Jesus"* (Philippians 4:6–7). This is a wonderful thought. God will watch over us even in our thoughts. So much of God's Word tells us we were not made for time, but we were made for eternity. So we must make our choices in view of the final end of this life. Eternity is forever, and God's purpose for us was to be with Him in heaven. We have all of eternity to celebrate the victorious day with Him.

I would like to tell a short story here: When God made Adam, He made him from clay, and He "*breathed into his nostrils the breath of life and man became a living soul.*" And from that, God created. It was God's "breath of life" that made Adam a living soul.

> *And out of the ground made the Lord God to grow every tree that is pleasant to the sight, and good for food; the tree of life also in the midst of the garden, and the tree of knowledge of good and evil.*" (Genesis 2:7)

Then God gave Adam a wife. She was formed from a rib from his side, to be equal with and protected by Adam. God named her Eve because she was the Mother of all things. (Genesis 2:9)

She and Adam were set in the garden of Eden and had a free choice. Both did what God told them not to do. They sinned, but they knew their choice was not what God wanted for them. After they sinned, Adam and Eve could not stay in the garden of Eden. Adam had to work for everything. That is the *beginning* of "our story" here on earth.

When we die, if we are saved by Christ, our souls will go to heaven forever. There is no death there. Christ is the answer for us now. God gave each one of us a soul. It is our choice to accept Jesus before we die and our soul leaves the body. Sin came in with Adam and Eve's choice to disobey God. Jesus Christ came to take the world's sin on the cross. Remember our soul never dies and lives on eternally. God wants to redeem His people from sin. That is why Christ died on the cross. Jesus Christ took all sin on Himself so that we might be saved. Every choice we make leads to another choice. We live here earth. What we do here with our choices counts when we leave this world. Eternity waits. God's plan of blessing and redemption is made available to us all.

God established a covenant and said he would bless all the nations of the world through His Son, Jesus Christ. He alone has the power to intercede on behalf of sinners. Jesus is the only one who has that power because of His death and resurrection from the dead. *Salvation is available to us now, by faith in Jesus.*

Jesus and Muslims

In 2011, I went to Israel again. While in Bethlehem, I started talking to a Muslim man. I openly asked him, "Are you Jewish or Muslim?"

He said, "Muslim."

Then he asked if I was a Christian, and I said, "Yes."

This opened up an opportunity to talk to him about the beliefs we both have. He said, "We serve the same God."

To this, I replied, "Your God has no salvation. You work for your rewards. Jesus took sin on Himself that *all* may be saved. Your prophet Mohammed said he was still looking for the light, that he was not the light, and to build no monument after him. My Jesus said He is the way, the truth and the light and no one comes to the Father (God) but only by Him (Jesus)."

This man and I talked all the way back to the tour bus. I do not know what happened after we parted. I planted seeds of the gospel in the conversation we had. I said a prayer for this Muslim man and asked God to grow the seed of faith that I had planted.

I know Muslims fear hellfire and purgatory. They know they do not live up to all of the requirements of their faith. A Muslim believes he must suffer for his own sins. If he thinks about another religion, he thinks he will suffer eternal punishment. I believe God will use what I said and will grow seeds of His love in this Muslim man. There is an entirely different meaning behind his religion, and they cannot understand the meaning of our Lord's salvation. Muslims believe Jesus is a prophet. However, when I asked, "Why don't you believe His words? You believe Jesus was a prophet because Jesus was the one who said He is the way, the truth, and the light, and no one comes to the Father (God) but by me," the Muslim man didn't know what to say to that. Even now I pray God will send other Christians to plant more seeds that this man, and others of his religion will know the truth of the gospel and accept Jesus Christ. Everyone who comes to Christ needs encouragement to become a part of fellowship with other believers. They also need to get into a church for their spiritual growth. Plus Christians need to read the scriptures daily to bring spiritual growth into their lives. They also need the Holy Spirit operating in their life every day, helping in their daily walk with the Lord enabling them to live a victorious life for Christ.

Every place I go now, especially since I've grown old, I still talk to people about Jesus. I have been talking with an elderly man who works at Wal-Mart. Every time I see him, he comes over to me and talks. I am planting seeds of God's Word every time we talk. Please pray for this man at Wal-Mart. When I see him now, he starts asking me about Christ. It has piqued his mind and he's been thinking about what I've told him. I know because he's asking me questions about my faith.

There is nothing to compare to the joy of when you win someone to the Lord! Try it and you will like it, I promise! *"Let your light so shine before men, that they may see your good works, and glorify your Father which is in Heaven"* (Matthew 5:16).

I love seeing God's Spirit move. Peter preached on the day of Pentecost, and three thousand people came to know the Lord! The joy there would be if we could see this in our witnessing to the many people in the world today.

I believe sin has reached such a level people can't tell the difference between right and wrong. Sooner or later the wrath of God will be poured out on the earth. Sin is wide open now and can be found everywhere.

TV brings many sins right into our front room. Selfishness, cheating, hating, lying, murder, gluttony, homosexuality, debased lust, and sex. All of these and more are sins God hates. Mankind's sin has affected all of God's creation. Even Christians are watching sinful things and are becoming morally corrupt. It is a documented fact many supposedly upstanding men, calling themselves Christians, are steeped in pornography. *We know judgment is at hand.* God is going to judge this world. Read Isaiah 13:9. Judgment is coming. This is not a myth. The details of this judgment are written in the Word of God. References to judgment are in both the Old Testament and New Testament. Peter preached at eleven in the morning, and three thousand people came to know the Lord! What joy there would be if we could see this in our witnessing! For the many people in the world today, I believe sin has reached such a level that they can't tell the difference.

We are seeing signs that indicate judgment is getting closer every day. Birth pains of it are upon us, but even greater pains lie ahead for the unsaved and for those who have rejected Jesus. This will be terrifying news. When life is over, there will be no more opportunities to come to Christ. When Jesus comes back, He will be riding at the front of the army of heaven to fight against sinners of this world.

We need to be compelled to share Christ with everyone. The good news is what He died for, so *all* could come to accept Him. He is warning people of today He is coming! We must ready ourselves. Meanwhile, we also need to tell others about Jesus. God said He gave people over to unclean minds through *"the lusts of their own hearts, to dishonor their own bodies between themselves"* (Romans 1:24).

> *Who changed the truth of God into a lie, and worshiped and served the creature more than the Creator, who is blessed forever. Amen. For this cause God gave them up unto vile affection: for even their women did change the natural use into that which is against nature. And likewise, also the men, leaving the natural use of the woman, burned in their lust one toward another; men with men working that which is unseemly, and receiving in themselves that recompense of their error which was met.* (Romans 1:25-27)

God is talking to sinners and to homosexuals. God loves every person, but hates the sin we have. It dwells in our flesh. God can give us a new heart to serve Him. *We just have to ask Him into our hearts.*

> I speak after the manner of men because of the infirmity of your flesh: for as ye have yielded your members servants to uncleanness and to iniquity unto iniquity; even so now yield your members servants to righteousness unto holiness. Holiness is living right and sinless before God. When you sin, repent quickly to be holy before the Lord God again. For when ye were the servants of sin, ye were free from righteousness. (Romans 6:19–20)

God wants us to be free from sin and to become servants to God to be holy and to have everlasting life.

"For the wages of sin is death; but the gift of God is eternal life through Jesus Christ Our Lord" (Romans 6:23). The Word of God (Bible) is life. We study it because it teaches us the ways of the Lord. God knows our thoughts and they are vain. We are so smart sometimes, yet we think vain thoughts. God knows all things even before we think them.

> *But the natural man receiveth not the things of the Spirit of God: for they are foolishness unto him: neither can he know them, because they are spiritually discerned.* (1 Corinthians 2:14)

> *Let no man deceive himself. If any man among you seemeth to be wise in this world, let him become a fool, that he may be wise.* (1 Corinthians 3:18)

Learn God's Word. When we apply His Word to our hearts, we overcome sin.

Our mind is where evil and good comes in. When given over to what our mind tells us, we sow to the flesh. When we feed on the Word of God, we will yield to good in our minds. God said to *"study to show thyself approved unto God as a workman that needeth not to be ashamed"* (2 Timothy 2:15). When we do this, our minds will know what is good and right and do what God wants us to do.

The Bible tells us in Ephesians 2:2–3:

> *Wherein time past ye walked according to the course of this world, according to the prince of the power of the air, the spirit that now worketh in the children of disobedience: among whom also we all had our conversation in times past in lusts of our flesh, fulfilling the desires of the flesh and of the mind, and were by nature the children of wrath, even as others.*

We are saved by grace through faith and not of ourselves, it is God's gift to us. In times past I've been told, by people I witnessed, why they could not live a Christian life. They would say things like, "It's too hard," or "I like to party too much!" They did not understand that God will give you new and better wants and desires if you will accept Christ Jesus.

"*The eyes of your understanding being enlightened: that ye may know what is the hope of His calling, and what the riches of the glory of his inheritance in the saints*" (Ephesians 1:18). That is us! We are the saints because we are believers! He will help us grow every day!

Tom and Rosemary

In the summer of 1970, Patty Ward and I were sitting in the Lee Hotel having dinner in the Chinese restaurant. On the other side of the hall of the restaurant, there was a bar and dance hall with live music on weekend nights. We were talking about events of the day, when a man came out from the bar on the other side. He just walked over and sat down at our table. He said, *"My name is Tom, and would you ladies like to have a drink?"*

I spoke up and said, *"Sorry, we're born-again Christians, but thank you. We would like to tell you about something better than a drink. That is Jesus."*

The three of us talked for two hours just sitting at that table. At the end of the second hour, he had given his life to Christ. We also told him we would go with him to Victoria, Canada on Saturday to talk with his girlfriend about Christ. Her name was Rosemary. (Port Angeles, Washington, United States of America is eighteen miles directly across the Straits of Juan de Fuca, from Victoria, Canada. You can only get there by ferry boat.) The Black Ball Ferry would leave Port Angeles eight-fifteen in the morning, and we would arrive in Canada around ten-thirty that Saturday morning,

Tom said, *"I'm going to rent a car for the day so we can spend the day here. I'll take you girls out to lunch also."* Things were going great and we talked of God. We went to Rosemary's house and to meet her. I believe she didn't know what was going on. She was dressed and ready for anything. Later she said she just didn't know what was up with Tom and the two women who said they were Christians. She also said that at first she thought we weren't for real. She truly didn't know what kind of women we were.

As the day went on though, we got to know her, and she got to know us. She believed us to be real. By early afternoon, we had also led Rosemary to the Lord. She was baptized in the Holy Spirit! She was telling us of a Pentecostal Church and the pastor named Hal Bredison. That was the first time I had ever heard of this pastor. Rosemary invited us to spend the night, so the three of us made arrangements to do so. Tom got a room at a B&B (Bed and Breakfast), and we settled in at Rosemary's house. We talked half of the night away and also talked to Rosemary's mother. When Sunday morning came, we all hurried to get ready for church.

We got to church, and it was already full of people. I was glad to be there meeting the family of God. We started singing songs we all knew, and you could feel God's Spirit falling on us like a blanket! In between the singing, there was praise! The Spirit of God was moving on everyone there. I had never felt anything quite like this before. Oh! It was so sweet I started to cry. The sweetness of God was there. Everyone was singing in tongues all at once. My! I can't tell you how beautiful this was. It was like hearing angels sing all in perfect chords. The worshiping of God continued with everyone singing, and God moved on into healing. The praise was so wonderful! This was the first time I had ever seen praise turn into worshiping. God was blessing everyone. The blanket of God's Spirit was so heavy, there were people laying down, sitting, and all worshiping God with everything in them. If you ever get a chance to be in a service like this, you will remember it for the rest of your life. When you come into a service like this and you have sold out to God, it is the most wonderful thing you can feel while you are alive! The glory of God is all around you. The power of God is there! You watch and anything can happen. You can feel and see God's power. Get in on it and get a big blessing. Feel and see what God has for you.

Hal Bredison, and his wife, became wonderful friends to us in Christ. His understudy youth pastor also became close to us. We were going over to his church once a month working to bring souls to the kingdom of God together. They were coming to Port Angeles, working with us. We were like family, pulling together for our Lord, winning souls in both the United States and Canada! International!

Coffeehouse in Port Angeles

By the end of January of 1970, I was back in Port Angeles, organizing a work for Jesus on the Olympic Peninsula. The following is an article published January 29, 1970, in the Port Angeles Daily News.

"Former 'Dopers' Plan Aid" By Flynn J. Ell

Twenty-four former "dopers" or "addicts" and concerned non-users in Port Angeles have banded together to open what they call the Reach Out Inn Coffee House. The coffee house will serve as a gathering place to "turn kids on to the Lord," explained Mrs. Nan Lundgren, who authored the idea and is herself a former "doper." By definition, an addict is "hooked on the needle" and a doper "drops acid, or takes speed," she added. Buoyed by their own experiences, in which the reformers claim they "turned on to Jesus Christ" through the Bible, the group plans to reach out to help others. The Reach Out Inn will operate Friday night in the basement of Mrs. Pat Ward's home on West 9th Street. Coffee and donuts will be served free and a musical group will provide entertainment. "Table talk religion" will also be served to those with an appetite for it in an effort to turn others on to Jesus. The reformers say coffee houses of this type are springing up throughout the nation as young people attempt to release themselves from the bonds of drug abuse. Port Angeles is no exception.

Five years ago Mrs. Lundgren had her first contact with drugs here when a girlfriend turned her on with marijuana. Until a year and a half ago, she joined in many Port Angeles parties on drugs brought in from Seattle. The reformers claim that 80% of Port Angeles young people, 14 to 24 years old, have had some contact with drugs. They dispute the opinion of any local officials who deny drugs are easily obtained in town. "We know who has got it and how much is out there. Who's going to tell a cop?" the reformers said, in forming a consensus. Statistics only show who got caught. Older people and the law don't know what's going on, they claim. Methods the reformers use to skirt detection of their drug supply included eating it, flushing it down a toilet, or stashing it on the outside ledge of a window where it could easily be pushed to the ground. The Rev. B.W. Ellsworth, of Evangelistic Chapel, who is a non-user associated with the reform movement, tempered the judgment that the law was ignorant of the problem by emphasizing the difficulty in detecting drug abuse. The law does what it can do. Mrs. Lundgren described a past scene. "We would buy a kilo of marijuana in Seattle for $200, stash it in the woods in Port Angeles and divide it into 65 lids at $15. Then the stuff would be sold until the original $200 was regained, then the rest would be given away. We wanted to turn on everybody in town," she said. The reformers say the full range of drugs are available locally. Tom L., age 19, said he was hooked on morphine and speed until he came off through "the power of the Lord." Tom said he began reading the Bible after his mind and body were *"burning up" from the effects of drugs he was taking. Miraculously, he stopped taking the needle-administered doses and his mind cleared.*

The reformers claim no one can really kick the habit without Christ. As Tom also said, "You'll always have that monkey on your back without Him—Jesus Christ."

Years have gone by now and many of us are still bringing souls to God. In the late '60s and '70s, there were many that would be saved in one day. The harvest is still there but the people of God are not sowing the seed (the Word of God) for the lost souls to hear and be saved. God will always use us if we tell people of his saving power. God's love is the highest of grace in understanding and all we do for Him.

Sequim Car Wreck

May 5, 1971, God gave me back my life back from a fatal car pileup.

About fifteen miles East of Port Angeles where I live, heading home (on Hwy 101), we were stopped for a wreck on a bridge, just outside of Sequim. There was a backup of five or six cars ahead of us, and we were the last vehicle in the line. Unknown to all in the lineup of cars waiting, a drunk man by the name of Layman was speeding toward us at 75mph in an old, heavy car. All cars were completely stopped, waiting for the highway to be cleared when he came flying over the crest of the hill and plowed right into the back of our car! It folded up like an accordion. There were five people in our car. Two of my sisters, my nephew Keith, my baby daughter DaLasa, and myself. My baby was thrown out of the car on impact. Out of six cars that were stopped in front of us, four were totaled. Later I was told I was the only person who had died. All four EMTs checked me, and I had no pulse. They thought I was dead, so they covered me with a sheet and left me to attend to the others. There were many injured and many ambulances were taking people to the hospital.

As they started to lift my body onto the gurney to take me to the morgue, several EMTs heard me begin to speak in tongues! They didn't know what it was and thought I was a Catholic sister speaking Latin! As God would have it, the last ambulance driver was a friend I had known since the '60s. They immediately jumped into action, stabilized me, put me into the ambulance, and rushed me to the hospital, not the morgue!!

The next thing I knew of anything that had happened was when I woke up in the hospital three weeks later! I began going in and out of consciousness for a whole month. Occasionally I would think of a few things related to the accident or wonder how my family in the wreck were doing. I remembered I had been on the roadside covered with a sheet. I remember seeing Jesus in a shape of a man but like a waterfall in front of me. I couldn't see his face, but I knew it was Christ. He was wearing a white robe. He spoke to me and said: *"My daughter you are not going to die yet. I have work for you to do."* Then I began speaking in tongues.

Finally, about middle of June, I came too and stayed awake. I looked at our mountains to the south. They were a beautiful, shinning pink. I said, *"Thank you, Jesus, for this view, it looks like snow cream on the mountains, all lit up and pink with color.* Then I saw Jesus again, standing next to my knees. I was on my back, one arm raised up hanging in a brace. I couldn't move. Once again He spoke and said, *"You will walk again."* Then he was gone. At that time, Drs. Had told me I would never walk again. Within a week I was in a wheelchair, getting in and out of bed with help!

Once again, my sister Cotha came to take care of me and my family. She did that for two years. She would come to my home for the week and go to her home weekends. Cotha's husband was an ironworker on another job building a dam, in another state. My baby girl DaLasa that was in the car wreck with me had head damage. My sister Margaret, also in the wreck, would be in a wheelchair the rest of her life. I had nerve damage in my back. Something had pulled away from my spine, my pelvis was broken in four places, a part of my system called "the dorsal tubular cord of nervous tissue" was hurt, and my right arm had compound fractures and was told I might never walk again. Boy, did I know they were wrong about that! I knew I would walk again! Jesus had told me I would!

Within a year, I was back on the streets witnessing for Jesus! The old devil hits us when God is using us! This is why we must fill our heart and minds with the Word of God. My God once again raised me up from death to life. If anyone ever tells you that *God, in Jesus, is the light,* believe them. He is. *This I know!*

The Bible says *we can do all things through Christ which strengthens us* (Philippians 4:13). God will build up our spirits as we grow in Him. God will always help us in everything we do for Him. For it is God that works in you. Both for His will and to do of His good pleasure. So press forward to the mark, the prize of the highest in the calling of God in Christ Jesus.

When He saved us and filled us with the Holy Spirit, He gave us the power for healing deliverance in Christ. We as a nation believe in God. But He wants to be Lord of our lives every day in our walk. If a blind man leads another blind man, won't both fall into a ditch? (Matthew 15:14). There are a lot of people wherever you might go that are falling into a ditch. The world is full of hate. We see it around us every day. As God's people, if only we could come together, let go, and let God! I have seen many different kinds of sickness and all that matters for healing of sickness and deliverance from demons is having Christ. We as a nation believe in God. But He wants to be Lord of our lives, every day in our walk on earth. There are a lot of people out there that are not sure and are still afraid to commit to Jesus. I'm telling you that people have to be blind to deny the existence of our Creator. He can be seen everywhere—in the mountains, the hills, the sky, the trees, the sun, and moon. He is everything we see and in everything we look at.

God wants to have communication with us. He loves us and wants to have a relationship with us. Jesus's sacrificed for us, showing God's love to us. Sometimes we have to sacrifice to show our love for Him. When we do, our relationship with God will flourish.

Remember, religion is not a relationship. Religion is going through rituals out of duty. God doesn't like religious activity. He wants a personal relationship with His people. He wants us to have a deeper walk with Him. Communication will bring us closer to Him. Open up your heart and ask Him in, He will hear you. Jesus says, *"Behold, I stand at the door and knock: if any man hears My voice and opens the door, I will come in to him."* Communication is our lifeline. It is called prayer. Talk to Him every day. Read His Word and know you will grow in the Love of God. He will show you His Hand in your life. Jesus said in John 10:27, "My sheep hear My voice and I know them, and they follow Me."

He also said when we go to Him, we will go in and out in fine pasture. Our lives will be full of joy and peace that will not be like the world. Our hearts and minds can rest in Him and know He is watching over us. This is an exciting miracle in itself.

God performs in our hearts and minds so we will not have to examine the mystery of the miracle God has done for us. You will know when you are born again in Him. *Your thinking will be only on the things He puts there.*

Your heart will want to tell others about the news of Christ. He has incredible love for *all* unsaved people. This all unfolds as you walk with Him.

In Romans 9:20–21, Paul was willing to give up his own salvation for others to be saved. This is a unique calling on Paul. Before his salvation, he was a killer who had been hunting down Christians to kill them. God came to him in a bright light and his life changed. From that time on, he loved and labored for God until he died. His conversion was dramatic and incredible. God wants all of His children to continually be His hands.

Responsibility falls on us all to tell others there is salvation in Christ, our Savior. When we go and preach, there is unbridled joy bubbling throughout your entire body. You can also have massive waves of praise and thanksgiving through your heart, knowing you are doing our Lord's will.

One time when I prayed, I expressed I was willing to go to hell for more people to get saved. Jesus spoke to my heart and said, "*That is why he died. I was just to tell others about His saving grace.*" In the '60s and '70s, the whole world looked like it had lost its moral center. I wanted to tell everyone what I now had in Christ. If everyone would reach out and find God themselves and mean it, He would come into their heart! God would become real to them. Just by asking Him into their heart and to forgive them for all of their sins, He would. We simply have to choose.

1972 Expo

June 12 to 17, in 1972, the date of a huge expo at the Dallas Cotton bowl. A music festival of Christian Music with Billy Graham and Billy Bright preaching. The press was calling it a "Christian Woodstock." My heart really wanted to be there with the Jesus army and work with them witnessing for Christ in.

I began talking about it to my friend, Pam Holtiling, and we began making plans to attend the event. The next thing I knew, my twin sister Ann called and said she was going with us to drive! Plans progressed, and in the middle of the week we headed to my sister's house in Dallas. This event marked the height of the Jesus People Movement, and I wanted to check it out downtown. Knowing I was actually there, an energy was springing up in me at a high level. My excitement was growing, so I hopped a bus one afternoon. I knew something good was going to happen as I went closer to the Cotton Bowl and began to meet some Jesus people. They told me about a coffeehouse where witnessing for Christ was being done. I no sooner got there when I approached a young man, about twenty years old, and began talking to him about Jesus. Within ten minutes, I had led him to Christ. There were two other people witnessing to a young lady next to me. They were praying with her, leading her in the sinner's prayer.

Saturday morning we all piled into Ann's car and went to the freeway near downtown. The people of Dallas had closed the highway June 17 for nine hours, and the Jesus Music Festival began!

Chris Kristofferson, Johnny Cash, Willie Nelson, and Pat Sirisena all performed. What a blessing! Saturday evening, the Cotton

Bowl was fully packed with eighty thousand people, all loving God, singing and worshiping Him as one! We were all handed candles. Next we used our lit candle to light the next person's candle all over the stadium. Then Billy Graham had all of the stadium lights turned off. You could only see this multitude of lit candles. Then they played the song: "It only takes a spark to get a fire going. You want to pass it on." We were all emotionally involved in the music and the high energy from the presence of the Holy Spirit. It was wonderful! We were sharing Christ's presence, and we were lifting up each other in prayer and deed. This candlelight service was wonderful to feel, see, and hear with eighty thousand people all holding lit candles. It was producing so much excitement in all of us feeling and knowing God's presence was there.

A renewed vision was in me. I so wanted the world to come to know Christ. I wanted a bigger spiritual revival for the world. I prayed for hours in the morning. I prayed for revival, I prayed for the world, and I prayed for souls that were dying, not knowing Christ.

There was a great mobilizing effect of Expo '72 that will live on in my heart for as long as I live. Sharing Christ and lifting others up is the vision we should all have. The activity of the Jesus People Movement was in everyone. You never met any strangers involved in the movement. We told everyone we could about Christ as we wanted everyone to have a spiritual birth. The only requirement to enter God's kingdom is to accept Jesus! Remember, "it only takes a spark to get a fire going."

As individuals and as a movement, we wanted and needed to "pass it on." I would like you to know what the coffeehouse in Dallas looked like. It was very different from the one we had in Seattle, Washington. The coffeehouse in Dallas was like entrance into a tent of Arabian Nights. Soft fabric was hanging on the walls, beanbag chairs were everywhere, and people were sitting around with coffee or tea. Everyone from the movement was working! Souls that came in as sinners were leaving with Christ! The love of Christ was profound and could visibly be seen whenever anyone asked Jesus to come into their heart!

This mobilizing effect of Expo '72 will be with me the rest of my life. I didn't enjoy the many famous people's singing nearly as much as I enjoyed bringing souls to Christ. I truly enjoyed working with the Jesus People Army! By the way, I got to meet Johnny Cash and the rest of the stars. I talked with them for fifteen minutes or so about Johnny's salvation, and that was very rewarding!

Bremerton

In the 1970s, on some weekends, many of us would drive to Bremerton to see my friend Linda Meisner. We enjoyed seeing God's children working in their coffeehouse and worship center. Linda couldn't always be there because she had a ministry still going on in Seattle, which is a ferry ride away from Bremerton.

What a wonderful movement that was. We were watching God do miracles every day. Sometimes I was so full of God's presence and the joy that comes with the fullness of the Holy Spirit, I wanted to go see Christ right then and there.!

We can miss God's will if we are not careful. We must look to God for our direction and answers every day. Just know that when we are happy, the devil will try to take us into the mindset of a storm. *The devil is always ready to mess with our heads.* One time, on the one-and-a-half hour drive back to Port Angeles, my mind was going over a lot of bad thoughts. God is so good. He turned me from my bad thoughts and mental anguish out of love, and gave me a verse! *"Fight the good fight of faith, lay hold on eternal life, where unto thou art also called, and hast professed a good profession before many witnesses"* (1 Timothy 6:12). That was deeply grained into my soul. Every day since then I've wanted to tell everyone Jesus is real! And He is! He wants us to come to Him in prayer. With our whole heart open to Him, and with our hands, so that he can use them any way He cares to use them. Be a light for all to see around you! Only then will you really know what it is to be a Christian. With the joy that comes with this, we can miss God's will if we are not careful. We must look to God for our direction and answers every single day.

Elwha Pastor

In the 1970s, so many people were getting saved, and many of these new believers were also getting delivered from drugs and alcohol.

I had a friend named Julie. She knew a man that had pastored the Indians on the Lower Elwha. She went to him and he agreed to be our pastor. Once again, God answered our prayers. In one week, we had a building and enough chairs for a hundred people to sit in. Oh, how good God is!

There are many different tribes of Indians around us. West of Port Angeles, an hour and a half drive away, is a tribe called the Makah. It is a self-governing, sovereign nation within our nation. The Makah were originally head hunters. At one time, they had the largest reservation in the state of Washington. They're the one tribe that governs itself without interference from the state of Washington. Federal or government agencies/officials cannot legally go on Makah property (for any reason) without the tribal nation's permission.

The Makahs have a special, white sandy beach called Shi Shi Beach. It is known as one of the most beautiful beaches in the world. When the tide comes in on starry nights, it's truly spectacular! My husband and I used to drive to the beach just to watch the water roll in, especially on stormy nights. People cannot pick up anything that comes in on the water. It belongs to the tribe. There is a large fine if someone does. Also, no one can be there at night unless a Makah native is with you. If you want to take something from their beach, a native also has to give this to you after leaving the beach. Even a piece of driftwood.

Other tribes in this area are the Hoh and Lower Elwha. These are small tribes. To the east is Jamestown, and Klallam tribes even smaller yet. All tribes in Clallam county are related Klallam tribes. However, each are self-governing, and each run their own gambling casinos. The combined tribes employ 100's of people, both Native and non-native, and are continually improving their environs.

Our Peninsula #1

The Olympic Mountain Range lies directly behind and south of Port Angeles, running east and west. We are blessed to see snowcapped mountains and tall, beautiful, evergreen trees everywhere you look. There is great beauty. Directly in front and to the north is the Strait of Juan de Fuca. Twenty miles from ski level to sea level. There are many rivers to fish and abundant hunting for deer, elk, and bear. West of us, the beautiful Sol Duc Hot Springs is in the Olympic National Park. Another beautiful place that stands on its own merit. Also within its boundaries is one of the most beautiful, deep, aqua-colored lakes in the United States, and some say the world, is Lake Crescent.

To the north, across the Straits, accessible only by ferry is Vancouver Island. Three hundred miles around, it is actually in British Columbia, Canada. Victoria, a seaport on the Island, is a picturesque, old English city. It is a tourist trap, especially in the summer. It's like being in a new and an old world at the same time. On Vancouver Island, fifty-five acres of floral beauty is the Butchart Gardens. A married couple by the name of Butchart started this beautiful place in 1904.

Every day all we have to do is to lift our eyes. Here we see so much beauty, and here we experience God and the wonder of His creation, right here on the Olympic Peninsula!

The observation tower from our city pier has a view of the mountains, harbor and Mount Baker. As far as you can see in any direction is beauty. We have short-term moorage for boats in the summertime and enjoy seeing all kinds boats, including the ferry, going out and coming in to moorage. We have a low crime rate here, however, drug dependency seems to stay in our county, as it is everywhere now days.

As we worked with the Jesus People Army, we saw the Lord's hand moving every day. I remember a man by the name of Roy Huhn, so demon possessed, he often upset our meetings. Our pastor said we should all fast over the week from this Sunday to next Sunday. We would all start ministering deliverance to him the following Sunday. He had many demons! They talked and told us they were not coming out! They made sounds like animals. We made sure no children were present as we stood in Jesus's name and casted them out. It still took us about thirty minutes, but he became free and was a new person in Christ. He was fully delivered, and he looked like a different person after his deliverance. Then he was filled with the Holy Spirit. Praise God! Later my husband and I worked as co-ministers with him in jail ministry for fifteen years.

Roy had many demons. Let's talk about this. There are people that go to church and are halfway sold out with God. They do not know that hanging onto many of their sexual, unclean sins, fears, hatreds, lying, smoking, or drinking are actually demons. Most people hang onto them because they like them. In this case, they cannot be delivered from them. Bear in mind that demon deliverance is not for amateurs. Christians must be fully committed and filled with God's Holy Spirit of power and wisdom. This is *not* something Hollywood invented. *They are real.* Unless God shows you a possession is there in the human, stay away! I have seen this often. You must be filled with God's Holy Spirit when this happens. When demons come out, some smell, some cry, some vomit or make guttural sounds and refuse to come out! Some make a loud, deep roar! Always remember, it is not you they come out for but the name of our Lord, *Jesus*.

Jesus said in Luke 11:24 that a demon would go to an unclean house (a human), not a home and live. God gave us the power in His name to deliver a person when we have been baptized with His Spirit (Mark 16:17). A delivered person can live the rest of his life in Christ and be happy and saved. We saw this many times working for Christ with the Jesus people. When Roy was set free, he was a powerhouse for God. He had a full life working for God. Roy married a lady named Judi. She would go into the jail each week and cut hair for everyone that needed a haircut. I know this because my husband and I worked in the jails with them for fifteen years. They would come and talk to us about Christ.

At Christmas time, My husband, Daryl and I would make up a clear bag of "goodies." Two pounds of loose candy, fruit, candy bars, a Bible, and a tract for each prisoner. When we were done ministering, each prisoner that came received their bag of goodies. Some Christians today have never seen anything like that in their walk for Jesus. My husband and I made over 145 bags for the men and women in that prison. We also prepared Christmas gifts for their children and delivered those directly to their homes. The happy faces of the children was wonderful to see and gave us great joy! Sharing the gospel with them was our life as God was always on our mind and something God put in our hearts. We understood when others had no mental understanding. God called us to do this and also anointed us regarding how to do it. Year after year, for fifteen years, the four of us labored and saw many prisoners (and others) come to God.

Judi, my friend, has a beautiful singing voice. Before she was saved, she sang in night clubs for a living. Now she sang for God. After she sang two or three songs, you could see faces light up. Some prisoners would then want us to pray with them. We rejoiced together for the sweetness of the Lord as they came to Jesus and lives were changed.

Some Christians who have been in church the most, some all of their lives, have never experienced any of the things God has promised to *all* who are His children. I believe He wants His children to do what He has called us to do, *according to what He said in His Word.* There is no joy like watching God's hand move on people when *His Spirit moves*! Healing, filling them with the Holy Spirit and *all* the works of His hands. I love a live church where God moves on everyone. Many Christians have never seen this. Some have but think it is weird or fake and that it goes far beyond their system of belief and sensibility. They are truly missing out on the blessing of God and what He has for them.

My Children and I 1989
Trina—David
Top—DaLasa—Scott—Me

Grandpa and Grandma Callicott 1900

THROUGH DARK CLOUDS SHINES HOLY LIGHT!

Susan Viginia (James) Callicott
Born April 3, 1847

Callicott Stables 1901

NAN HEATHERS

Nan, and Daryl Heathers in Hawaii

A close friend questions response to fatal fall

THROUGH DARK CLOUDS SHINES HOLY LIGHT!

Kathy—Nan Heathers

Daryl, Gold Panning $6000 of gold
(Heathers 2002)

Ann and Nan at 16 years old

Ann Horton and Nan Mills

THROUGH DARK CLOUDS SHINES HOLY LIGHT!

Nan Hardy—Ann Hardy

Nan—twin's Ann Hardy

CC WOM OLYMPIC MEDICAL HOSPITAL	HEATHERS, RITA NAN
939 Caroline Street	MRN: 60003263193
Port Angeles WA 98362-3909	DOB: 3/7/1939, Sex: F
	Adm: 5/9/2015, D/C: 5/31/2015

Right internal jugular central venous line.

Left-sided chest tube.

Peripherally Inserted central venous catheter (PICC).

Imaging studies (see below).

History and Hospital course:
76-year-old woman with a history of recurrent atrial fibrillation underwent ablation treatment at Virginia Mason in Seattle a few days prior to admission. This was her 2nd ablation procedure. It was complicated by right phrenic nerve dysfunction. Patient presented to hospital with shortness of breath, and was diagnosed with a suspected aspiration pneumonia. She had a moderately elevated troponin level. She did not report chest pain. She did have an abnormal electrocardiogram, with anterior T-wave inversions, in normal sinus rhythm. Her case was discussed by telephone with on-call cardiologist at Virginia Mason. The troponin elevations were attributed to the ablation procedure. The patient was admitted and started on antibiotic treatment for the suspected aspiration pneumonia. The next morning a follow-up electrocardiogram showed larger amplitude T-wave inversions and QT prolongation. The patient had remained on monitor for atrial fibrillation post-ablation. That morning the patient had a cardiac arrest. She was shocked out of ventricular fibrillation. She subsequently developed a torsades pattern polymorphic ventricular tachycardia, and was shocked out of that. After transfer to the critical care unit she subsequently had a PEA cardiac arrest. In that context amidst other standard interventions she underwent a pericardiocentesis emergently, without significant fluid returned, and without subsequent evidence of any major pericardial effusion. Resuscitation was successful. The patient was maintained on ventilator support. He began to wake up in the midst of these events new left-sided weakness was noted. There was question of a small left pneumothorax on chest x-ray, and challenging ventilation, and CT chest subsequently demonstrated a large anterior pneumothorax. This was treated with chest tube placement.

The patient stabilized on the ventilator, albeit with pulmonary infiltrates and continued antibiotic treatment. She required fairly substantial oxygen. She seemed to do well on spontaneous breathing trials, but failed extubation on 2 occasions, each time developing accelerating distress in the context of chest pain and increasingly rapid and labored breathing. She had considerable chest wall tenderness. She was subsequently left on the ventilator for a longer period of time with a slower approach to weaning. She eventually sufficiently improved to allow extubation to temporary BIPAP support for one day, and then made steady progress.

The patient was significantly encephalopathic in the wake of these arrest events. She had confusion and spells of severe anxiety, as well as left-sided paralysis. I actually, she has had gradual and very substantial improvement in mentation, and very substantial improvement in left-sided strength. Her left hand is not quite normal yet, but dramatically improved. Her left leg still drags and is weak, impairing but not preventing limited assisted ambulation with a walker so far. Patient's excellent progress to this point is encouraging with respect to longer term prospects for more complete recovery. In addition to the weakness, the patient's much improved mentation may not be completely 100% yet. I don't think she is back to her usual self, nor does the patient. She has been troubled by

Sister Arminta

THROUGH DARK CLOUDS SHINES HOLY LIGHT!

Cotha—Margaret—Wylodean
All off Mothers Girls

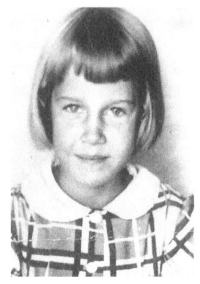 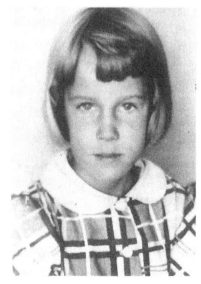

Nan Hardy   Ann Hardy

Great grand father Hardy

Downtown Iuka Ms. 1900

Watermelon in back of truck
Daddys cotton field 1942
The watermelon came out of cotton field

1954
William E. and Julia D. Callicott children

Grandfather Hardy with Daddys Family 1908

Bill of Sale for slave

Milton—My dead brother—At smoke house and the corn crib

THROUGH DARK CLOUDS SHINES HOLY LIGHT!

My sons Scott and David Mills

1955 Ann—Nan Hardy   Nan—Arminta—Ann 1944

Cousin's eating watermelon

Clothes collection show

THROUGH DARK CLOUDS SHINES HOLY LIGHT!

Daryl Heathers

Dad—Clyde feeding a Bear

Aulton and potatoes pickers

THROUGH DARK CLOUDS SHINES HOLY LIGHT!

Margarett and Aulton (Jack) Hardy
1950 shipping out

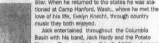

Lord on February 16th, 2005. He was born in Luka, Miss. on Sept. 18, 1930 to Clyde and Viola Hardy along with six sisters and a step-brother.

Jack was a Tennessee Walking horse trainer in his late teens before he joined the Army. He served in the army infantry in Korea as a Corporal receiving a Purple Heart, a Silver Star and a Bronze Star. When he returned to the states he was stationed at Camp Hanford, Wash., where he met the love of his life, Evelyn Knecht, through country music they both enjoyed.

Jack entertained throughout the Columbia Basin with his band, Jack Hardy and the Potato Pickers. They married on Feb. 2, 1952 and shared 53 years together. They have three daughters, Sandra, Julianne and Wendy. They settle in Warden, where he help developed some of the land which was put into the Columbia Basin Irrigation Project. In a few years he became a farmer and agricultural field representative until his retirement. He then enjoyed spending time with his family, working in his yard and doing wood working in his shop. Jack loved children and stretched his helping hand as far as he could. He coached Little League and always bought milkshakes when they lost and milkshakes and hamburgers when they won. He was a member of the First Presbyterian Church. He was a beloved husband, father, grandfather and great-grandfather.

His family was very important to him, as he was to his family and he will be deeply missed. He is survived by his wife, Evelyn; daughters Sandra Allred (Skip) Snohomish, Julianne Sullivan of Warden, Wendy Gilbert of Moses Lake and Bill Gilbert; grandchildren, Bart, Chad and Brandy Allred, Stephanie Reitz, Crystal Sullivan, Heather Abregana (Jason), Halley and Brandon Gilbert; great-grandchildren, Mackenzie and Jared Parker, Sierrah Allred Benjamin Sullivan, Allison Abregana and Corben Reitz.

Services will be held at 10 a.m., Saturday, Feb. 19 at the First Presbyterian Church, 1147 Ivy Street, Moses Lake. Viewing will be held one hour prior to the service at the church. Interment will be at Sunset Memorial Gardens in Warden.

Brothers Death

Nan Heathers Scottsdale AZ.

Me in Scottsdale AZ.

THROUGH DARK CLOUDS SHINES HOLY LIGHT!

Me in Israel

Hawaii—twin Ann—(Sonny) Horton

Johnny Cash—Jesus people 1972

Jesus people 1972

THROUGH DARK CLOUDS SHINES HOLY LIGHT!

Expo Jesus people Texas 1972

Texas Jesus people 1972

Go-Go—Dancers 1964

Nan—Ann—in Jr. High School

THROUGH DARK CLOUDS SHINES HOLY LIGHT!

Betsy our cow, Ann and I

Ann Daddy Mother Me
Wylo Dean—Cotha—Margarett—Aulton—Arminta

Med 20's Daddy and His Girls

Daddy 1918

Daryl Heathers—200 and falling tree

Hardys fete anniversary

1971

Surrounded by all seven of their children, 15 grandchildren and five great-grandchildren, Mr. and Mrs. A.C. Hardy of Gales Addition celebrated their golden wedding May 5.

This was the first time all the family had been together in more than 17 years.

Mr. and Mrs. Ralph Lee with Sarah, Bobby and Karen came from Forks.

Mr. and Mrs. Mike Neely came from Pomeroy, Wash. Mr. and Mrs. Bruce Little came from Springfield, Ore.

Here from Warden, Wash., were Mr. and Mrs. Jack Hardy with Sandra, Julia and Wendy.

From Heidelberg, Germany, were Mrs. Arminta Wyatt with Mary, Joe, Donnie and Ronnie.

Mrs. Ann Horton and Keith came from Tacoma.

Others were Mr. and Mrs. Dave Lundgren with David, Trina and Scott; Mr. and Mrs. Jim Lee with Toni and Jamie; Mr. and Mrs. Gary Monnot with Cindy and Gary Jean.

MR. and MRS. A.C. HARDY

Mother and Daddy 1971

Husband and I diving

THROUGH DARK CLOUDS SHINES HOLY LIGHT!

Diving lessons

A friend Duane starks

Diving with friend

October 14, 2017
My DNA

THROUGH DARK CLOUDS SHINES HOLY LIGHT!

Kathi Rolley and Nan Heathers model some of the vintage dresses to be on view at 'Vintage Memories' fashion show.

Aulton C. (Jack) Hardy

Aulton C. (Jack) Hardy, age 74 of Moses Lake went to be with the Lord on February 16th, 2005. He was born in Luka, Miss. on Sept. 18, 1930 to Clyde and Viola Hardy along with six sisters and a stepbrother.

Jack was a Tennessee Walking horse trainer in his late teens before he joined the Army. He served in the army infantry in Korea as a Corporal receiving a Purple Heart, a Silver Star and a Bronze Star. When he returned to the states he was stationed at Camp Hanford, Wash., where he met the love of his life, Evelyn Knecht, through country music they both enjoyed.

Jack entertained throughout the Columbia Basin with his band, Jack Hardy and the Potato Pickers. They married on Feb. 2, 1952 and shared 53 years together. They have three daughters, Sandra, Julianne and Wendy. They settle in Warden, where he help developed some of the land which was put into the Columbia Basin Irrigation Project. In a few years he became a farmer and agricultural field representative until his retirement. He then enjoyed spending time with his family, working in his yard and doing wood working in his shop. Jack loved children and stretched his helping hand as far as he could. He coached Little League and always bought milkshakes when they lost and milkshakes and hamburgers when they won. He was a member of the First Presbyterian Church. He was a beloved husband, father, grandfather and great-grandfather.

His family was very important to him, as he was to his family and he will be deeply missed. He is survived by his wife, Evelyn; daughters Sandra Allred (Skip) Snohomish, Julianne Sullivan of Warden, Wendy Gilbert of Moses Lake and Bill Gilbert; grandchildren, Bart, Chad and Brandy Allred, Stephanie Reitz, Crystal Sullivan, Heather Abregana (Jason), Hailey and Brandon Gilbert; great-grandchildren, Mackenzie and Jarad Parker, Sierrah Allred Benjamin Sullivan, Allison Abregana and Corban Reitz.

Services will be held at 10 a.m., Saturday, Feb. 19 at the First Presbyterian Church, 1147 Ivy Street, Moses Lake. Viewing will be held one hour prior to the service at the church. Interment will be at Sunset Memorial Gardens in Warden.

In lieu of flowers, contributions may be made to the First Presbyterian Church Building and Scholarship Fund.

A Man Called Clarence

When God wanted me to start working with the Jesus People Movement on the Peninsula, I never once asked if it was in the Lord's will. I only knew I had a drive deep within me to see people come to know Jesus Christ and be saved. It is still there.

One night, eight of us were going out to witness. We paired up, two-by-two, and started out, heading to night clubs, restaurants, and streets, looking for people anywhere that would talk to us. Patty Ward and I started at the Lee Hotel night club. We were handing out tracts (pamphlets that tell a short salvation message) and started talking to people. We handed a tract to every person sitting and drinking in the bar.

A young man named Clarence took a tract and greeted us with a smile. I knew he was different from most of the people there but didn't know just what it was yet. He told us later he was a pastor's son of a small church here in Port Angeles. A short time later, we got to see Clarence come back to God and take a stand for Christ. He is serving God again, pastoring somewhere around the North Seattle area and has a lovely wife by his side. She helps him with the pastoral work. How proud his dad was of his son. We knew then it was worth handing out the Christian tracks. Clarence's dad, a godly man, who taught me about the blessings from God, has gone on to be with the Lord. Clarence went into the service for three years, serving our country overseas. He is now home, preaching the gospel, doing the <u>will</u> and the good pleasures of our Father in heaven.

Battle of the Mind

The Word of God tells us it is appointed once to die. Then comes judgment. We will all stand before God at the judgment seat of Christ.

If you are not saved, hell awaits. The fear of God keeps you alert in your body, soul, and spirit when you are saved! (Matthew 12:3). However, sooner or later we will *all* stand before the judgment of Christ. At that time, He wants to welcome us into His kingdom. He died for *all* people. We have to come to the wonderful realization of the wonderful freedom in Him. *If we abide in Jesus we will enter into rest in Christ. He will give us peace* (John 14:27). Christ says: *"Peace I leave with you, my peace I give unto you, not as the world giveth, give I unto you. Let not your heart be troubled, neither let it be afraid."*

God's peace is this: rest in Him, and *He will be there when you are in trials.* He is there in all the storms of our lives. We can be victorious and stand strong for Him during each trial. We can take control of our mind, and Christ will be there. The battlefield is in our mind with the devil, but God is *always* present in our hearts and minds. Ephesians 6:12 says: *"For we wrestle not against flesh and blood, but against principalities against powers, against the rulers of the darkness of this world, against spiritual wickedness in high* places." In the storm of the adversities and in the solving of problems, we stretch our Spiritual wings. You can't become an overcomer if you never have anything to overcome.

Remember, we only have our minds that come with good and evil. Arm yourself with the Word of God. This *is* the ammunition that gives us "good" (or God). If we recognize that the battle we fight *is* the devil, then we can have freedom in Christ. We can then live life with purpose and greater goals. The motivation is with God in the center, watching the effects as we walk with Christ and share his word. People will see we are Christians when we are being true witnesses for Him and sharing His love with others. The public will know we are serving God. When we serve God with love, all motivation is God centered. We will not always be able to stay happy with circumstances in our lives, but we can have peace, if our mind stays on Christ. We will know heaven awaits. We cannot control everything in life, but we can control our life to come. Heaven or hell? In fact, we are the only person that can control and determine where we will go eternally. God awaits and watches over us here. We will reign with Him when we leave this world. We determine our own fate by our choices here on earth. We cannot blame anyone else for the position we have chosen in our lives. *We are the only one that can do this.* Only while we live can this be done. It is too late when the body is dead. It is in our own hands in all we choose to do in this life. God has made the way for us to make our way back to heaven and live with Him forever. Jesus took our sins upon himself, so we might have forgiveness of all of our sins. This means all sin, not part, but all sin.

The Peninsula

The Pacific Northwest has so much to see. The Olympic Peninsula has more beauty than anywhere else in the world. I have never seen such beauty any other place I have been, and I have been around the world. The forests, rain forests, contrasts, and ecosystems are uniquely their own here. Just fifty-four miles away is the town of Forks, known as the logging capital of the world. Timber reigned supreme.

In Port Angeles, the harbor ranks among the world's three finest, deep-water harbors. The Olympic Discovery trails are nearby and cover many miles. There is a low crime rate among the twenty thousand residents.

The entire area is full of beauty with so much to see and to do. As a small town, there is a lot to enjoy, especially in the summer. Port Angeles, surrounded by the Olympic National Park, is filled with wonderful, sweeping views of mountains, foothills, rivers on two sides, and not far away, two beautiful lakes. The Olympic Range towers behind us, protecting us from storms, etc. It protected our peninsula from the ash fallout of Mt. St. Helens volcanic explosion. There is a mountain or water view from almost every house in town. On a clear day, you can see Seattle from the summit of Deer Park's mountain. Halfway up the mountain to Hurricane Ridge, one can see seven counties, the city of Bellingham, Washington, and the lower northwest corner of the continent of Canada. From Port Angeles, the Straits of Juan de Fuca. On Hurricane Ridge (a world famous destination), one can even see a glacier. There are guided auto tours through the Olympic National Park. In the fall, we have Salmon and Halibut

Derby Days at The Spit, a natural five-mile long, finger of land that defines our beautiful, deep inner harbor. This two-day event offers cash and other prizes. Years ago, Port Angeles had the largest Salmon Derby in the world. People came from all over the world to participate. Fishing and tribal regulations have curtailed most events. There is also a National Wildlife Refuge that is an awesome place to see. God has truly blessed all who live in this wonderful place.

Many movies are filmed here with historical and educational value. I have worked on movies filmed here and even talked to movie stars about where their souls would go when they died. I am sorry to say I did not bring any of them to God. Sometimes we can only plant or water the seeds of salvation, but we can sure plant! We must tend the "garden of life." Quite a few movie stars live or have summer homes here. John Wayne had a house and even invested in a bank here. He came with his boat, The Wild Goose, which he moored in a marina here summers. His sister still lives in the area, next to the water, year round.

As a little girl, I loved John Wayne and watched his movies. John was born May 26, 1908 and was named Marion Michael Morrison. John Wayne is his movie name. I wonder about his soul. I do know his family that goes to my church, which I've attended church for over 50 years. John Wayne visited here a lot and enjoyed the beauty of the Peninsula. His family is a wonderful, sweet family. Barbara Streisand also lives here in the summer with her husband. They love the green trees and the beauty. I have never met these people personally, but sometimes a helicopter with her last name on the underside goes over my house. The Bionic Woman, Lindsey Wagner, along with many others, even comedians, live here unknown to the public. Lindsey Wagner has come back to the big screen in a new DVD. Just released May 2019, it is called *Sampson*.

In the '60s, I knew just about everyone. Anywhere I went, I knew people. There were only about ten thousand people here then. Now there are many I don't know. However, it is one of the prettiest "green" places to live all year around. People are moving here from all over the world, and we all feel the same about this incredibly, wonderful place.

A Tale of Four People

Here is a little story of four people, named Everybody, Somebody, Anybody, and Nobody.
There was an important job to be done, and Everybody was asked to do it. Anybody could have done it, but Nobody did it. Somebody got angry about that because it was Everybody's job. Everybody thought Anybody could do it, but Nobody realized that Everybody wouldn't do it. Consequently, it wound up that Nobody told Anybody, so Everybody blamed Somebody.

Here is a true story on YouTube that completely exemplifies this story of anybody could, nobody would, even though everybody was screaming for help from somebody. Somebody finally did and saved the day for everybody! At a brand-new Detroit Zoo enclosure, a male chimpanzee fought a smaller ape, who then fell into the deep moat surrounding the enclosure. The smaller chimpanzee was drowning. Zookeepers were looking on, but nobody made a move to save the little guy. Park attendees were screaming for them to help, but still nobody moved. Finally, somebody (a man) in the crowd jumped over the fence, into the moat, saved the little chimp, and barely got out with his life just as the large male ape almost reached him! Later the man was hailed as everybody's hero but did not think he was one. He said, "Anybody could have done it, but nobody did, so I did! Somebody had to do it!" Look it up, it's a great story. All caught on tape. Thank God for the "somebody's in our lives!"

That can apply to most of our lives if we don't do what God has called us to do. The world will call to us, and we need to make sure we're arming ourselves with the Word of God, with praise, and with prayer. These are powerful spiritual weapons! Feeding your mind with scripture is important so that you can recall them when you need them. We must know that in our mind is where we make warfare with the world. God on one side wants us to grow spiritually. The devil on the other side wants us to have selfish thoughts. He fills our minds with depression, doubt, and condemnation, always attacking our mind. We must gain control and find the freedom in Christ. Then we can live a victorious, wondrous life while we are being transformed by the Lord.

Ephesians 6:13 says to put on *"the whole armor of God that ye may be able to withstand in the evil day, and having done all, to stand"* (so we may stand against the "wiles" of the devil). "Wiles" in the dictionary means devious or cunning strategies employed in manipulating or persuading someone to do what one wants. To fool, entrap, or entice—*that is the duty of the devil!*

We are also told in the Bible to put on the shield of faith, the breastplate of righteousness, the helmet of salvation, the sword (Word) of the Spirit, and to gird our loins with truth and to shod our feet with the gospel of peace. That is the *full* armor of God!

1982 Trip: Israel, Kenya and Beyond

In 1982, a friend and I were talking about going to the Holy Land and were hoping someday God would make a way for us to go.

The very next night, our pastor told us the 13th World Pentecost Conference was to be held September 13 in Kenya! We began immediately planning to attend that event and then go on to the Holy Land! We were blessed when booking the trip as it included five countries in fifteen days! Kenya, Africa was our first stop. I can't tell you how exciting it was to me!

At the World Pentecost Conference, we met people from all around the world. Many would say, "*Hallelujah!*" when they put out their hand to shake ours! "Hallelujah" means the same all over the world! As we took their hands, the word would come enthusiastically two or three times with a huge smile! Everyone's mind was on Christ Jesus. I had great joy hearing the African choir singing in their own language. Everyone was so blessed!

Their traditions and culture were very interesting. We visited a tribe outside of a city in Kenya and had the pleasure of watching a traditional dance. Homes were mud huts with grass roofs. Living in America, I cannot imagine living as they do. Reflecting on a vivid, mental picture of the simple mud huts and smells of that place, I cannot begin to imagine living there. I will never forget that experience, and I will never forget how blessed I am to live here, where I do!

The Christian conference was an emotional, inspiring, wonderful experience. I met many people who came from all over the world. I met and led a sweet lady from the Bomba tribe to the Lord. We wrote each other for years after I came home. Her baby was named

Collin. I loved that little guy and sent him clothes from America. I did this until he grew up and became a man in his twenties. Always, I will remember that trip to Kenya. September 15, we went on a safari. I was ecstatic to be able to see so many different animals. The physical excitement of seeing such large groups of wild animals was palatable! As we watched them, running in herds of so many different kinds, I was filled with complete and total awe!

On one particular day, it was getting close to lunchtime. We arrived at a camp set up with a lot of tables and box lunches for everyone. As we were eating lunch, a "troop" of baboons came up to us. Our group started feeding them the apple cores and anything else they would take and eat. I had already eaten my food and apple and just put a piece of gum into my mouth. Just then a smaller baboon came up to me, and with his big brown eyes, he was begging me to feed him. His eyes got to me, so I handed the gum to him and he put it in his mouth. He chewed it twice, then it came out of his mouth. I said to him, *"I'm sorry. Here, I'll pick it up for you."*

As I picked it up, he bit me twice before I could pull away! I yelled really loud the second time he bit, and the blood started flowing! The driver of our safari said I would have to get shots for rabies! *Yikes!* A hundred and forty-two cases of rabies had been confirmed that month alone from animal bites.

I heard myself saying, *"Oh no! Only me!"* as the driver said, *"We have to go now!"* Off we headed to the Kenyan Hospital where I was given treatment. Rabies shots were new and had just arrived over there from France. The first three days, I had a shot in each arm and a shot in each upper leg, followed by one day of rest. Then I had to return and repeat the four-day routine for two whole weeks. By then I would be in Egypt! The medicine had to be packed in dry ice for safe keeping until I could take my next shots.

Israel

The Holy Bible is not the entire history of the house of Israel. But rather it is the history of God's dealing with His people in Israel.

Archaeologists are finding more and more artifacts confirming the Bible is accurate. Experts are finding real evidence that the Bible *is* a true account. The Bible is so accurate that its texts are always current and never need to be updated. Discoveries have only served to confirm the truth and accuracy of every story in the Bible. Research absolutely backs up the biblical stories which helps these stories come alive. Documents and artifacts are being uncovered that are like breaths of new life coming into the ancient texts! Each discovery brings new and deeper understanding of the Word of God. Discoveries are continuing to shed new light on how people lived back then and is giving and creating a more complete picture of the ancient world. Evidence is being shown to the world and is available for everyone to see. *People can also know God is real if they will just receive His truth.*

Excavations of ancient sites are being uncovered every day that confirm biblical truths. They confirm, without a shadow of doubt, the Bible is the true Word of God. I pray that God opens all eyes to this understanding so that people will know Him as their personal Lord and Savior. We are so very close to Christ coming back to get His Church. Not the name tags over the doors of each church building, but His church body of true believers in Jesus Christ. These are the born again Christians. They are His chosen body that is fully serving Him in their hearts and minds.

> There was a man of the Pharisees, named Nicodemus, a ruler of the Jews: The same came to Jesus by night, and said unto him, *"Rabbi, we know that thou art a teacher come from God; for no man can do these miracles that thous doest, except God be with him."* Jesus answered and said unto him, *"Verily, Verily, I say unto thee, except a man be born again, he cannot see the kingdom of God."* (John 3: 1–3)

God has been dealing with mankind from the beginning, starting with Adam and Eve, and all of civilization that has come afterward. Christ came and died on the cross. He died so that we might have fellowship with Him once again. We will never fully realize the love He has for us until we see Him. God wants us to receive Jesus first, then He wants us to go and evangelize the world, telling other people about Jesus and His salvation that is available to *all* of us!

Standing on the Mount of Olives in Israel, looking at Jerusalem, the holiest city of the three greatest faiths in the world—the Jewish, Muslim, and Christian faiths. Here, tradition is rich with the biblical accounts we know. Here, Abraham came to sacrifice his son Isaac, and God provided a ram as a substitute. Here, Solomon built his temple for God. Here, the queen of Sheba came with her caravan of camels, loaded with spices, gold, and precious stones to visit Solomon in his kingdom. Here, Christ Jesus came during the last days of His life on this earth. Here, Jesus prayed in agony before His crucifixion. Here is the garden of Gethsemane where olive trees were all around me. My heart was full standing in that place. Yet looking over toward Jerusalem, I saw the gleaming Dome of the Rock of another faith where Solomon's temple once stood. I began to tear up knowing that Christ knew what was about to happen to Him. His divine authority and His death was for *all* men! It all began. *Here*!

The Valley of Kidron was below me. There I saw the grave of King David's son and the graves of many Jewish people also. I knew that many had missed the calling of God when Jesus was nailed to the cross. *The journey of the Word of God truly began here.* Memories of treasured Bible stories were stirring and filling my head. Being there is so sweet! I sensed the power of Rome and began thinking of all the olive trees cut down by the Romans to hang more than five hundred people a day on crosses. The olive trees have now grown back. All of Israel is deeply rooted spiritual soil, yet many ancestors and people living right now, right here, *do not know that Christ died for them.* I felt the presence of Christ very strong there as God continues to guide the destiny of His people, the Jews. The course of history is still changing and happening today in Israel. Bible scripture is being read all over the world. The precious manuscripts are being translated and written in every tongue and language. Every country in the world now has access to the Bible. Israel is where places of the Bible are visited by tourists every day.

A popular tourist destination, Megiddo, is the valley where the last war in the world will be fought. Armageddon of the Bible was Solomon's chariot city. Bethshean is where the head of Saul, Israel's first king, was displayed by the Philistines on the wall with his sons. The Philistines conquered them, took their armor, cut their heads off, then hung them on the wall for all to see (Samuel 31:10). Christian stories come to life, and there is a quickening in your faith! I have been to Israel more than once and even at my advanced age, I would go again if I could. My heart longs to be in the New Jerusalem with Christ and is why I love visiting Israel so much. In biblical times, a dangerous route to travel was the old Roman road to Jerusalem that rises into the Judean hills (Mark 10:24). Jesus used that as the setting when He told the parable of the Good Samaritan. In the outer part of the temple, Jesus drove the money changers out. He rebuked them for making God's "house of prayer" into a den of thieves (Matthew 21:13).

The only remains of Herod's temple at Jerusalem is the Wailing Wall. For centuries the Jews have come here to mourn the destruction of the temple that occurred in 70AD. Today, not only Jews but people from all over the world come to worship at this revered and sacred place. The bustle of city life is all around in Jerusalem. Pickpockets will try to take your wallet if you are not careful, yet an air of religious excitement is all around. Upon entering the Dome, you have to take off your shoes to walk on the plush, rich-colored red rugs. In the center is a massive rock on which Solomon built his temple. Earlier in history, Abraham was going sacrifice his son Isaac here. Nearby is the Via Dolorosa, "the way of sorrows." It is hallowed as the place Jesus carried his cross and is also the location of His entombment. Being here is like being in a living museum that is preserving timeless sites. This is the place of "the Upper Room" where Judas slipped out into the night to become Christ's betrayer. The Upper Room, where one hundred and twenty people, including Jesus's mother, Mary, were filled with the Holy Spirit! They all spoke in tongues as the Holy Spirit gave utterance. Nearby is Gethsemane. There Jesus prayed on his last night on earth. In this prayer He said, *"Father, if Thou be willing, remove this cup from me: nevertheless not my will, but Thine be done"* (Luke 22:42).

Jesus knew He was going to die. It was the spring season of the Passover. It would be Christ's last time in His life that He would be in Jerusalem for He knew the cross was awaiting Him. Christ knew we would come to know Him as our personal Savior. *Christ is the only one that is the truth and the light.* We *must* go through Him to enter Heaven when we die. Christ wore the crown of thorns for all of us. Above His head on the cross, a sign had been nailed that said: "King of the Jews." Only by the sacrifice of Jesus, the Christ was the great door opened for *all* to be saved. For centuries, pilgrims have journeyed to Israel hoping to know more about Christ and what is ahead for all Christians.

I may have left Israel but I left a part of my heart there. After the visit to Israel, I read the Bible with new life because the stories literally jumped off the pages as I remembered standing in the very places they named and described. Those stories never get old for me or anyone. The love I have for the Word of God grew after seeing and walking the land of God. Remember, our beloved Creator God created you for Himself, and He wants to have fellowship with you.

"Know ye not that your bodies are members of Christ?" (1 Corinthians 6:15). *He is our Maker, and He loves all of us.*

Greece

Greece, beautiful Greece! Athens was full of life with sidewalk cafes, Turkish coffee, arts, and museums. Athens is also the fountainhead of philosophy. Greek Athenians still cling to the teachings of Socrates, Plato, and Aristotle. Oh, and how I enjoyed the incredible architecture and sculptures. Today, Athens ports still remain the rendezvous of sailors and travelers. On the water, one sees small and large vessels rolling over the sea, hauling goods from sea to sea.

Here, Paul spoke of the unknown God on the rock called Areopagus or Mars Hill (Acts 17–18). Here, Paul preached to the Athenians at the jewel of Athens, the Acropolis. Here, Paul won hearts to the Lord as he spoke to anyone that listened. Here, Paul baptized Lydia, the "seller of purple" who dyed cloth and sold it as a business. Here, Paul and Silas were jailed and freed by a quake. Here, they converted their jailer in Acts 16:25–34.

The food in Athens was very nice, very good, and fresh every day. We ate by seaside restaurants on the Mediterranean Sea. Yogurt, made from goat milk, fresh fish, goat, lamb, and lots of seafood. They have the best deserts in the world. The bread was thin bread with pine nuts basted in yogurt and butter. Smells of the sea and smells of the food were so notable that everyone in our group was talking about them. Some people in our group had never been to the sea shore until now. A boy, approximately eight years old, was fishing beside us with his homemade fishing pole. As we were eating with all of this around us, a seller of goods came over to our group and began telling us how much their goods were. Some of the handmade table cloths were extremely colorful and very pretty! You know I had to buy one! We spent three incredible days in Athens.

The presidential guard is something only seen there. Uniforms were thigh-high, multi-pleated, white muslin kilts, with a white blouse under black-and-gold embroidered wool jackets. Their caps were red, and the shoes adorned with pompoms on top. They held guns over their shoulders and were very colorful and impressive.

Piraeus, connected with Athens main harbor, is lined with open air cafes which is where we ate. To the west are the remains of the Hellenistic theatre and the museum. The yacht club is here. Fishermen in the many-colored fishing boats could be seen mending their nets, adding a touch of the islands of Athens to our view. That incredible visual, along with the smells of the sea, filled the senses. That is what I was looking for, as that is what I had been told the place was like! It was awesome being there and walking in the very places Paul walked and stood preaching. As I stood on Mars Hill, I closed my eyes and heard the words Paul preached from the book of Acts 17.

Petra, Jordan

Petra means "rock." This place was a wonder. The red color rock must be seen to be believed. The first impression of the strangeness of the place is felt when entering the city by horse, foot, or camel. It has the sensation of entering into another world. There is a narrow, sheer cliff as you go into the city of Petra that goes about a mile down a narrow passageway. No sound is heard except the pebbles under the horses' hooves and the wind. High cliff walls are on each side.

When we entered Petra, we could see part of the largest monument—the Khazneh. *Khazneh* means "the treasury." It is a preserved monument ninety-two feet wide and a hundred thirty feet high, with sculpted columns and is breathtaking. This awesome place was the great capital of the Nabataea's at the height of their power. They ruled the country as far north as Damascus. Occupied in the fifth century BC to the fifth century AD. Their heyday was the first century BC and AD, as there are references to the city of Sela, in the Bible. This name has the same meaning as Petra. *Sela* also means "rock." This place was is a wonder. We were told these people probably started as a wandering Arabian tribe that grew to have riches from the plunder of caravans from Arabia. The first historical mention of them is in 312 BC, when Petra was captured by the Antigones, and their great treasures were taken away.

The wandering of the Israelites and Moses stopped here. This is the place Moses struck his staff on the rock and water gushed out. Moses's brother Aaron is buried in a tomb here. It is a place of complete awe and overwhelming beauty. The theater, hewn completely out of rock, can seat about two thousand people. In the background, you can see the facades of early tombs cut away in making the theater, leaving the inner chambers open to sunlight. I appreciated the great wonders of the city and its lovely red rock and now recognize this place in many movies.

Switzerland

I was told Switzerland is the land of some of the best chocolates in the world, and I was looking forward to checking this out for myself. Our plane was twenty minutes from landing when the stewardess came around with a silver dollar-size chocolate bar for each passenger on the flight. What a nice surprise! It was wonderful, filling my mouth with creamy chocolate that melted as soon as you put it into your mouth. Landing in Switzerland was much like looking down on Seattle. It was green everywhere. To me, there is no place in the world more beautiful than where I live. The Olympic Peninsula in the Pacific Northwest. It will always be the most desirable place for me. However, as I looked around the countryside of Switzerland, I knew this was also a place where I could be happy living. It was so much like the greenery that I see living in Washington State.

Our group talked about going shopping when we got off the plane in Geneva. Many wanted to buy Coo-Coo clocks and mail them home. That's what everyone did. We loaded into the tour bus to see the sights of interest around the town. We saw the United Nations, the Red Cross, and where some movie stars from Hollywood lived. Of course, not one tourist in our group spoke their language. I went to a number of Swiss people and asked, *"Do you speak English?"*

"No, no," was the response from every one of them. Finally a lady spoke up and said she was from another country but could help all of us in our group. Wouldn't you know it, she was a Christian and stayed with us the rest of the day! What a joy she was and she seemed to enjoy being with all of us also.

Off we went shopping again to a different store that was wonderful! We left loaded down with gifts for home. Geneva's gardens and grounds were a beautiful picture in the city! I have never seen this anywhere else. Flowers were everywhere. However, I have no desire to go back there as I already live with this beauty and more here in Washington State.

Egypt and Going Home to United States of America

We were at the pyramids in Cairo, riding on camels. Nearby and to my left, was the Sphinx. The Sphinx is seven stories high and maybe a football field in length. I ran out of film in my camera, so I looked in my shoulder bag for a new roll of film. I reached into the bag to pull the film out, and my hand went on the medicine for my next shots! I pulled the medicine out. The dry ice was gone, and the medicine had turned bright blue. My last shots from the baboon bites in Kenya were due in four days!

We went on about seeing the pyramids. We were told they were ancient, even to Greek historians of the fifth century BC. These are marvelous monuments of unspeakable greatness and are estimated to have been built forty-six hundred years ago. Entrances had to face north, so they could make star sights. They cover thirteen acres each, with the average block weighing about two and a half tons. This alone is absolutely amazing. The Nile temples and tombs were also impressive and awesome! My head couldn't learn all of it fast enough. Cairo was flooded with tourists and trying to learn anything about Egypt was almost impossible. I took pictures, pictures, and more pictures. Hearing the wail of Arab music, shouts of vendors, smelling the smells of living animals, of roasting food, all mixed with the city dust and Nile mist, I had some sense of ancient Egypt.

I saw a woman with the beautiful features of Nefertiti. My mind went immediately back to a 1962 movie, with Elizabeth Taylor playing the part of Cleopatra with her dark hair. Cairo City was like that movie with the Egyptians and all their clothes hanging on fences. The museums of Egypt were crowded with treasures of the Pharaohs. I loved this city which was modern. Taxi cabs were going ninety miles an hour on the streets. They were going so fast that when the driver put on the brakes, you had to hold onto something or you would slam into the front seat from the backseat!

The memory of Cairo will remain in my mind a long time. Turkish coffee will always be there in my mouth. Oh my! It was such dark stuff and had an incredibly strong flavor! When I left, I was still thinking about all of it and wanted to see it all again!

The Bible has an account of baby Moses's early life in Egypt when the Pharaoh's daughter adopted him as her own son. Moses was learned in *all wisdom* of the Egyptians. As I went down the Nile River and walked on the land, I wondered if Moses had walked in that very spot. The desert stretched for miles. Many of the temples and tombs still stand and "speak" from Moses' day. History and science has certainly proved the truth of the Bible.

Now Cairo was behind me, and we were on the airplane going home. I had gone to the hotel before we left Egypt and told them my medication had "gone bad". I needed another round of shots and showed them the bottle the medication was in. They said when I got home, it would be taken care of. When I got to New York, I was met by a person who told me someone would be in Seattle to give me the last of my shots. When I got off the plane in Seattle, a man standing in lobby of the airport was holding a sign with my name written on it. He had come to give me the last of my rabies shots. France had shipped the medicine on an earlier plane while I was still in flight to Seattle.

The next day in the Seattle newspaper was a story of the first American to take the new rabies shots. The paper said she was bitten while feeding bubblegum to a baboon. I was happy they didn't include my name in that article! Once again, I knew God's hand was still on me. I look back on this now and laugh, but at the time I only wished it had not happened. I had so many shots over the two weeks' time. It was neither easy nor fun.

I had been bitten in Kenya, the thirteenth of September 1982. Now, all of the rabies shots were over. Truly, I left my heart in Egypt. I do long to go back there, but I know I never will. There is no other place in this world where I have been that had the feeling, smell, and lifestyle like the people of Egypt. I left there, not winning one soul to God. There were many that talked to me in English, and I did tell them about Christ. Now, I pray God continues to water the seeds I planted. There, the Pharaoh held the children of Israel four hundred years before Moses came and led them out of slavery. Then they wandered forty years in the wilderness, always looking back to Egypt. Yet, with all the wrong hope in their hearts, still God blessed them.

Soul Patrol

Daryl Heathers was my third husband, and I loved him dearly. He was very calm, kind, even tempered, and a cheerful Christian man. We were married in 1984. My first two husbands had passed away. One in the 1960s, the other in 1980. My husband, Daryl, carried a pocket full of gospel tracts almost all the time. A loving Christian man, he would go out on weekends to witness for Jesus with another brother in the Lord named Roy. Daryl called it their "Soul Patrol." They would go for about three hours then come home to tell their wives how many people they had prayed with and how many had asked for forgiveness for their sins. With happiness and joy, they would share their work of winning souls for the Lord each evening.

One time, we were driving east on Highway 101 and had just stopped at a red light. All at once, fifteen motorcycle riders came roaring up beside us. Daryl jumped out of the car and started handing out gospel tracts to them. On the back of their coats was "Hell's Angels." Daryl didn't seem to notice that at all. Some of the bikers even thanked him for the tract he handed them. Then the light turned green, he jumped in the car, and off we went! That was a nice thing for him to do and was a regular pattern in his life. Daryl and Roy went on "Soul Patrol" almost every weekend for fifteen years.

Daryl continued to do that until his tragic death, June 13, 2002. Daryl, my kind, loving husband that loved everyone and everyone loved back. A hard working logger, gentle soul reaper for God, loving husband and father, he was simply a man everyone looked up to. God must have especially loved him to take him home so soon.

He had been working on our roof, and it was hot out, so I had gone to town for groceries and lemons to make him lemonade. I arrived home to find Daryl had fallen headfirst from the rooftop, right onto cement bricks! He died instantly, his cranium broken open. A neighbor had covered him with a blanket. Ambulance EMTs found they could do nothing for Daryl. They called the sheriff, who in turn called the coroner and the mortuary. There had been a delay for various reasons of four hours. Four hours in which my family and I had to endure endless questioning while bearing the unbearable horror, pain, and tragic loss of our beloved. God is merciful. He blanked the horrendous devastation from my mind. Had *He* not done that, I do not believe my heart could have physically endured the pain of what my eyes had seen.

Mother-in-Law Anne

In 1987, my mother-in-law, Anne Baay, had a stroke. My husband Daryl came in and said his sisters couldn't take care of her. Daryl said he would like to take her into our home. Just five months earlier, I had put my own sweet mother in the ground. She had stayed with us for one year, and she had died of cancer. I had no idea what was going to be in front of us. My mother-in-law had been a drunk, although she had asked Christ into her heart. However, she was not completely into the Lord. Daryl also knew God was not finished with his mother. We had chosen to take care of her and knew God promises in His Word He will strengthen us and be with us in the time of need. We thought we were ready.

On February 4, she was moved into our home. She had Alzheimer's disease, and we had known this before she moved in. What a different world this disease is. Alzheimer's is a degenerative disease of the central nervous system, characterized by premature mental deterioration. Oh my, I could have never guessed what was to be ahead of us. Here was a trial that was not going to stop for the next three years we took care of her. I knew God had said, "*I will strengthen thee, yea I will help thee, yea I will uphold thee with the right hand by my righteousness*" (Daniel 2). I really leaned on that knowledge! Here I would say, every promise in the Bible is ours.

God can deliver us from all of our troubles. Cigarettes were just one of the beginnings of all the things we would have to watch for. One morning around breakfast time, I heard Anne on the telephone in her bedroom. I didn't know who she was talking to, so I put my head into the doorway of her room and asked, "*Who are you talking to, can I help?"* At the same time I knew something wasn't right, so I asked, *"Can I have the phone, Mom?"* She handed it to me. I asked, *"Who is this?"*

Their response was *"The taxicab service."*

"Was she ordering a cab?" was my comeback.

The taxi dispatcher said, *"No, she was trying to get me to go to the liquor store to get a bottle of alcohol!"*

I couldn't believe this. Now I had to take the phone away from her, only letting her receive phone calls. It was something we dealt with every single day. We had to take turns being with her for in just a matter of minutes she would get into trouble.

One morning, I was running out of things to cook. My husband said he would watch his mom for me. He said, *"Go get the groceries and supplies we need."* Off I went, thinking Daryl would be fine. I left in peace. I was gone for an hour and a half. When I pulled into the driveway, I saw smoke coming out the doorway. The firetruck and a police car were here. I got out of my car, thinking, *What? How can this be?*

As soon as I saw my husband, *"What happened?"* was out of my mouth.

He answered, *"I had to go into the shop for a few minutes. While I was gone, she set a fire in the kitchen, on top of the cupboard!"* Anne told Daryl she was camping and had built a fire for cooking!

Now we couldn't leave anything out anymore. If we did, it would take us a few days to find it. Always she would say someone stole her pack of cigarettes. She didn't smoke at all anymore as we had taken her cigarettes away months ago. She didn't know what she was doing most of the time. However, she was always very exact in knowing what she was looking for. Day after day, it was the same thing over and over. It seemed like the harder we prayed, the bigger the war. It was really getting bad. I would go upstairs, fall on my knees, and pray hard for God's help. He would be the best guidance to all of our peace.

We got to where we would pack up a few of her things and take her different places with us. That kept her happy for a while, but three years of that situation seemed like forever. Her walking had to come to a stop. Time and time again, we found her outside on the porch or in the yard or walking down the street with no clothes on. And I mean *nothing* on. Our neighbor would call us at one or two in the morning to tell us she was out on the street with nothing on. Off we would go to get her again. She would be so cold, I would have to give her warm showers to warm her up. We thanked God we only had to go through that a short time. Just before the three years were up, she had two more strokes and died from the second one. She died in peace and never knew her mind was gone.

In those three years, my husband and I felt like we were going to fold under taking care of his mother, but God was with us. Many times we couldn't feel God or feel His hand in our life, but we would praise Him anyway. As we praised Him more, our worship would begin. We would know for sure then that He was there all along. Sometimes, our minds would be far from Him, but at night, when things were quiet, we would know He was there waiting for us to come before Him. God wants us to prosper and be in health.

"*Beloved, I wish above all things that thou mayest prosper and be in health, even as thy soul prospereth*" (3 John 2).

We had been under a heavy load taking care of Mom for so long. Now we were coming up for air, no more negative thinking. We can build strongholds in our minds of faith. Know that God is a rewarder of those who earnestly and diligently seek Him. We should always praise and love Him. Not because we are trying to get something from Him, but because we truly do love Him. His Word does not lie to us—ever. Lean on Him and seek His face. You will find God is willing and able to answer *all* of your needs.

When circumstances become beyond control, turn it over to God. You know, "Let go and let God!" Stop trying to control everything that goes on in your life. Complaining makes us hard to live with and makes others miserable too. Humble yourself before God. God will reward you with love. Joy will return to you and fill you with love.

When I was taking care of my mother-in-law, I often found myself becoming frustrated and impatient with her. It became a huge

"*Oh no, God!*" Fleshly pride sprung up in me! At times I even lay in bed at night complaining to God. By using endurance and patience, we will accomplish what God's will is in our lives.

"*For ye have need of patience, that, after ye have done the will of God, ye might receive the promise*" (Hebrews 10:36). This is true. God was teaching this to me when I was taking care of my mother-in-law, Anne. Every day I would cry out to God. Keeping a good attitude was a *huge* trial for me. I would throw up my hands and quit on her. Once a week, I would say to my husband, "*Take her some place for an hour,*" just so I could have a little time of my own.

One morning, we rose early. She didn't look right and told us she was feeling bad, so Daryl took her to the doctor. They put her in a rest home for a few days. However, she never came home again.

A Fallen Tree

My husband, Daryl, worked in the woods as a logger. He was a timber cutter of trees. I prayed every day God would keep him safe while he was in the woods. Being a timber faller is not an easy job. Every few weeks or so, we would hear of someone being killed or badly injured in this line of work. Daryl was sixty years old at this time but still loved his work and did not want to quit. However, he was getting slower now, and in my mind, I was praying all the time for him.

One morning at eleven o'clock, the Spirit of God hit me. I began to pray in the Spirit *hard*. After a few minutes, the Lord told me it was my husband of eighteen years I was praying for! Daryl only worked six hours a day cutting, so I knew I would see him in one-and-a-half hours. I continued praying with no interruption. When I heard his car pulling into the driveway, my heart jumped, and I yelled out loud, "*Thank you, Jesus*!"

Daryl always came in the back door. He would take his cork boots off on the back porch, then off came his clothes, and he would leave them by the washer. I ran to him and asked, "*What happened at eleven o'clock?*"

He turned around and showed me his chest. It was black and blue. Then he told me his story. He had been trimming the limbs off of a tree he had just cut down when his boot slipped out from under him. He fell, with the chainsaw still running! He said the corks on his boots loosened the bark on the tree, which gave way. Down he went! As he was falling, he saw a broken limb aimed just below his heart! The limb hit his chest, turning it black and blue, but he was still alive! Praise God! Thanks again to Our Lord!

THROUGH DARK CLOUDS SHINES HOLY LIGHT!

God cares for everyone. To paraphrase, *"His eyes are on the sparrow and He watches over all of us!"*

When Daryl fell on that broken limb, he said it was like sawdust crumbling as he fell on it. As he went down, he shoved his chainsaw to the side of the tree he had just cut! That fast thinking saved him from death! He could have been badly cut by his own chainsaw while it was still running! He knew God had given him a miracle that day. The next day, back on the job, he showed his chest to his crew. They also knew God had performed a miracle for him.

At the end of his tree-cutting one day, a man came up to him and wanted to know what was different about him. Daryl turned his saw off and began to tell the man, Randy Hart, about salvation. That evening Randy went home as a saved man. He told his wife about his salvation, and a few days later she was in church and also saved.

Daryl's crew watched him walk a Christian life. Loggers are infamous for their "colorful language." However, they began to watch their language around him. He prayed each morning for the safety of the crew, and they also prayed with him. One day someone asked him to pray for their needs. This became more common. Every day, all of the crewmen he worked with, he prayed for. He did this gladly and loved it.

Once he had a large tree to cut down and was worried it would fall the wrong way. He wanted it to fall fifty feet *away from* the creek. Not close to the creek, nor into it. He walked around and around the tree, praying it would fall correctly. He knew if he put the undercut in wrong, a lot of money would be lost for his company. That would not be good. He began to pray again. He knew the tree was leaning to far toward the creek. He started the undercut and again prayed as he put the saw to the tree.

Randy watched Daryl walking around the tree, praying before he cut it. Now it was down, and right where Daryl had fallen it, fifty feet from the creek! Randy walked up to Daryl with a big smile and said, "*Yes! Daryl, that was great!*" Randy saw God's hand on this tree. He said it looked like God put his finger on the top of it and laid it down perfectly! Now his boss was pleased.

Daryl ended his work that day with much happiness.

Our Boat

One Saturday, we planned to take the boat out and anchor it in a suitable place where we could sleep for the night. Our boat was twenty-nine feet long and had enough room to sleep six people. We would often take it out to fish and catch shrimp for the weekend. This Saturday we anchored off a point called Dry Creek. It was a lovely day, and both of us looked forward to having fresh fish to eat. Two hours had gone by since we started fishing. Every fish we caught was too small, and we had to let them go.

Sunday morning came, we got up before sunrise and were going back into town to go to church. I said, "*Daryl, I'm going to put a line in the water and hope to get one good fish.*" As soon as I dropped my line in the water, I got a bite. I caught a 10lb. silver salmon!

My husband heated some water from the bay and boiled the fish. This technique is called "the poor man's lobster." What a wonderful breakfast we had that day: Fresh fish, eggs, and sour dough bread—all provided by God! God had given us a savory breakfast of fish to eat, and we were still on time to go to church!

I would like to share with you how we got our boat. And yes, once again God's hand was in this. My husband had been going down to the pier where the boats are all tied up, next to the boathouses. He saw a boat that was taking on water, so he went into the office and reported it. The pump was not working on the boat called The Hideaway. Daryl went back the next day, and the boat called the Hideaway was underwater. The owner of the boat was there this time, so Daryl began helping him bring his boat up out of the water. Daryl asked the man, "*Would you be interested in selling this boat?*" Since the boat had been underwater, the owner no longer had any interest in keeping it, so he said he would sell The Hideaway to Daryl! We got the boat for just five hundred dollars, and Daryl brought it home. He worked on it every chance he had until it looked new inside and out. It was a lovely boat when he was finally finished. Everyone from the boat harbor was telling him how nice it was. He said his boat had already been baptized, being underwater, so he renamed it "Born Again."

Daryl was walking on air, so excited, knowing God's hand had to be in all of this. He had prayed for a boat in the past, and now *God* had answered him! He shared his story about this proudly and frequently. Soon everyone at the Boat Haven knew that Daryl had prayed this boat in! On the fourth of July, we would take our boat into the harbor and watch the fireworks. Our whole family would pile in, and we would all enjoy the fireworks show together. We would even bring our little dogs, Bitty and Rascal, with us. We enjoyed many suppers in the evenings aboard the Born Again! Those were very good times!

(Addendum to *The Boat*)

In 1970, a Pentecostal man, the pastor of his church, wrote a song called "The Lighthouse." I love hearing this song at night, in my mind when I was lying in bed. I would hear the foghorn sounding off in the distance. It made me feel lonely inside hearing the sound. I lived next to the waterfront for over fifty years and loved every moment. It is a nice, easy, pleasant way to live, especially with the many blessings God has given to me. Some of the words of this song ring in my ear.

"There is a Lighthouse on the hillside that overlooks the sea. If it wasn't for the Lighthouse, where would this ship be? I thank God for the Lighthouse, I owe my life to Him. For Jesus is the Lighthouse and from this wreck of sin, He has shown His Light around me that I might clearly see."

Yes, the words of this song came to my mind at night as I listened to the foghorn blowing in the distance. It reminded me that Jesus is our lighthouse!

I believe all of our spiritual freedom was bought with a price on a hill called Golgotha (Calvary), with the death of Jesus Christ. He gave us authority with power to go minister to the lost ones in this world. God gave us a big world to look at. There are stars at night, and there is beauty in this world for our eyes to behold. We need to tell God, "*Thank you for the things we see and for all of the things that we receive from you. Oh Lord, Thank you!*"

Tent Fire

My husband Daryl had a hobby that both of us enjoyed. Gold panning! One day he came home from work. It was a three-day weekend, so he said, "*Let's go camping.*" We assembled our camping gear, grabbed the fishing poles, gold pans, and away we went to a good camping location. We were having a great time. I caught a nice fish to fry while he was panning for gold and was getting supper ready. He knew it and came into camp just as the sun was setting. So were the bugs and mosquitoes! There were so many we couldn't get away from them!

Daryl went into the tent, lit a lantern, and told me to come in. Just as I entered, the lantern fell. Daryl quickly picked it up and tossed it to the tent's doorway. It hit the screen and the side of the tent. Now the tent was on fire! He immediately put the fire out, but now there was a hole on the side of the tent, and mosquitoes were pouring in! I always left things like that for Daryl to fix. He took his shirt off, tore the back off of it, from the sleeves down, and made a flat piece of cloth. He took duct tape and taped the piece of shirt to the tent. That stopped the mosquitoes from coming in! Now we could enjoy a good night's sleep without a horde of mosquitoes pouring through the hole all night long!

We had a great time panning gold and fishing. Our three days just flew by, and we headed home, already looking forward to the next three day weekend. With our stomachs full of fish and $60 in gold dust in our pockets, we headed home! We were a happy couple!

God's Word and Salvation

In the book of Acts, there are many promises. God wants us to step out and be bold with His Word. Acts 17:26 says, *"And hath made of one blood all nations of men for to dwell on all the face of the earth, and hath determined the times before appointed, and the bounds of their habitation."*

That they should seek the Lord, reach out for Him, and find Him, though He be not far from every one of us. Think about this. God knows all things about us, even where we will sit when we go into His house to pray. He knows what we are going to do before we do it. Isn't that awesome? He knows all about each one of us. For the Christian, you could not want anything better than this.

"For in Him we live, and move, and have our being; as certain also of your own poets have said, for we are also His offspring" (Acts 17:28). This is awesome! He said we are God's offspring! My mind only wants more when I read things like this.

"For as much then, as we are the offspring of God, we ought not to think that the Godhead is like unto gold, or silver, or stone or graven by art and man's device" (Acts 17:29).

God "spoke: this world into being and made us in His likeness but with a man's mind. He even walked and talked with Adam and Eve and enjoyed their company. Then they walked away with shame in sin.

God put life and breath in all living things. Since Adam and Eve sinned, God commands all men everywhere to repent. God gave us this instruction in order that we can come back to Him with a repentant heart. To accept and believe in Christ is done by an act of faith. You hear the Word then "choose this day whom you will serve." Through your natural human mind hearing truth, a person realizes they have a desire to go to Christ and receive Him as their Savior. Then God speaks to your heart calling you to salvation. Believe what your physical senses tell you. You have everything to gain and nothing to lose. Respond to His calling and His love! Don't just act on your feelings, what the world tells you, or by what people may say to you. Get your Bible and begin by reading the books of John, Mark, and then Luke. The word of God will teach you what the Father wants you to do with your life. He has given it to us *all*. His book is for each of us to hold in our heart. The Holy Bible is the Word of God and are His promises. God put life and breath in all living things. Since Adam and Eve sinned, God commands all men everywhere to repent. God gave us this instruction so we come to Him with a repentant heart. To accept and believe in Christ is an act of faith. You hear the Word, you choose this day whom you will serve. Simple. Profound.

The Goal of Prayer

Prayer helps us establish the purpose of our lives. We must not lose heart. Praying is a place of power. It is the answer to all troubles and pressures. It makes life exciting, living daily with His power working in our life! We can face the pressures of life by trusting God for everything.

Prayer and faith bring us directly to God as we willingly open our hearts. We make contact with God when we pray.

Thessalonians 5:17 tells us to "*[p]ray without ceasing.*" God will change our attitudes from complaints and criticism to praise. This brings great joy into our lives every day. Prayer is just talking to God and pouring out our hearts to Him. He responds to us.

We as Christians need to be obedient to God in everything. We are to pray to the Lord with hope, faith, and forgiveness, never losing heart. Unforgiving is an unhealthy thing to have. As such, it can block us from hearing a response from the Lord if we come before Him in prayer with unforgiveness in our heart (Matthew 6:15). We must not carry an attitude of unforgiving when we pray. If we are offended by someone, forgive them. Immediately.

"In everything give thanks: for this is the will of God in Christ Jesus concerning you" (1 Thessalonians 5:18).

Often our lives are rattled by daily complications leaving one in need of patience. While this may come, it will take us to our knees in prayer and frequently conflicts will be resolved. Most of the time, hardships bring patience into our lives. Difficulties help us grow and learn to trust Christ more, teaching us to endure variable types of circumstances will be accomplished in us.

Over time, Jesus's name comes as naturally as breathing to us. Learning to pray to God, using His Word, will also become a natural part of our life. We use Jesus's name when we conclude our prayers. God honors His Word above all things. *"I will extol Thee my God, O King; and I will bless thy name for ever and ever"* (Psalms 145:1).

My friend Nina Fisher was my Bible teacher for nine years. She told all the ladies in our group to pray the Word. Over the years I have learned this is so true. How wonderful to pray His Word and watch His hand move in answering many of our prayers. We watched His power move in each lady's life as our requests and petitions moved our faith higher, and still a little higher. The Word says God dwells in praise and worship. This will deepen your walk with Christ. We had wonderful praise and worship times!

It is prayer that will carry you through death, divorce, cancer, big terrible things, and the smaller challenges also. God wants to commune with us daily through His Holy Spirit and through His Word. It will be impossible not to marvel when you look back at all the things you've come through. Look at all the circumstances only God could mend through answered prayer. We can have endurance because God is faithful to be with us!

A friend of mine, Shirley, was working long hours at a fishing Lodge in Alaska. Her boss kept adding more and more duties every day to her already full schedule. As manager, chef, dishwasher, and housekeeper for the entire lodge, it was becoming impossible to handle all of the work day in and day out. Conscientious and a hard worker, she tried to keep up but it was becoming impossible to handle all of the work day in and day out.

One evening toward the close of day, she walked out into the tundra to talk with God. Looking up at the heavens and talking directly to God, she said, *"God, you didn't bring me up here for this!"* Exhausted, she sat down on the grass and started crying.

Immediately, the *"peace that passes all understanding"* covered Shirley. God spoke audibly to her: *"I will give you wings to fly, you will run and not tire."* Knowing it was a verse in Isaiah, she ran back to the lodge, picked up her Bible and read God's word in Isaiah 40:31. *"But they that wait upon the Lord shall renew* their *strength; they shall mount up with wings of eagles, they shall run and not be weary* and *they shall walk, and not faint."* She finished the rest of the season with renewed energy, spirit, and extra help in the kitchen! That verse is very, very specific for *all* who labor and are weary. Often quoted, it is used by many, some not even Christian nor religious. The eagle is recognized everywhere as a vision of strength, great power, and endurance.

God is a god of wonders in more ways than one. He lacks nothing—not light, not insight, not power, not knowledge, not love. For He owns the cattle on a thousand hills. He possesses all things in all fullness. However, God desires for us to talk daily with Him. He wants to have a personal relationship with each one of us. He will talk to us also. This is a call to prayer. I read somewhere that a Christian only prays about three minutes a day! Wow! Only three minutes out of twenty-four hours!

"*I have fought the good fight, I have finished my course. I have kept the faith*" (1 Timothy 4:7). Spend your time and energy in the exercise of keeping spiritually fit. We only do that by reading God's Word and in our prayer life. If we don't, then trials will come and we won't know how to fight. We know trial build patience, making us stronger and teaching us that prayer and troubles do go together. We must always look to Him for answers to our petitions of prayer with thankfulness. Remember, when we give our hearts to Him, He call us to be faithful and to do His will.

My Fashion Collection

In the early 1980s, my friend Shirley had a catering and costume shop in Port Angeles. She had been doing teas for churches and private parties for years, and now it was becoming more and more popular. She had begun to dress her helpers in period costumes when serving, and women were enchanted with that. It is about that time I started working with and helping her. Another friend of ours, Carole also helped with teas, small and large dinners, and events. The High Teas Shirley catered were exquisite. People often commented they were as good, if not better than anything in New York society. She had an eye for design, placement, and beauty and was an excellent chef and baker. Shirley had a large amount of costumes, but her main interest was authentic vintage fashions. Her collection was quite extensive.

As we put on more shows for churches, teas, political events and such, we became well known. The interest and passion I always had for vintage clothing was growing with every show we did. We worked well together and had a lot of fun doing what we both loved. My daughter Trina, my son Scott, several of Shirley's daughters, and other friends modeled for these events. We were in pictured in the paper often as the combined occupation of costumes and high teas in an old western logging town was unusual. People began giving Shirley and I their great-grandmother's dresses, hats, and fashionable attire they didn't know what to do with.

However, Shirley's life was about to take a different turn. God had given her a message she was to move. She sold the bulk of her large animal (think Miss Piggy and Kermit, etc.) collection to a

Pentecostal Church in Victoria, Canada who had a huge children's ministry. (Her 'Miss Piggy' was called "Victoria La Swine.") As God had shown Shirley a new vision for her life, my life was about to take another turn also! She left her collection of vintage clothing and costumes with me! I was ecstatic! I Having begun to collect my own vintage fashions, and along with hers, I would continue the high teas and shows for churches where ever I was called. I also began to indulge my new hobby of sewing authentic reproductions for a more extensive collection—which in turn led to supplying a few movies made in the Pacific Northwest with my authentic costumes!

As a young girl, Mother had told me about the types of clothes my grandmother and ancestors wore. Mother would describe my grandmother's large home and how her large hoop skirts would reach from one side of the parlor to the other. Also, I loved watching movies with vintage fashions of years past. I was a teenager when I saw *Gone With the Wind*. That movie was filmed in 1939, the year I was born.

I loved the costumes and wanted to know why so many changes occurred in fashions over the years. Armed with Shirley's collection and mine growing steadily, I became even more curious. I had already been reading every book I could find on fashions. My thirst for learning this was insatiable. My hobby became sewing. I was able to repair vintage dresses and costumes with similar materials. My favorite outfit was a full-length cotton dress with a hoop skirt from 1864. From the mid 1980s and into the 1990s, I was giving fashion shows and telling about each particular style as we showed vintage attire on live models. We were having high tea parties all around the Pacific Northwest.

Years went by, and I found I had built a collection of more than two thousand pieces, along with a large collection of hats from different eras. At one show in British Columbia in Victoria, Canada, I showed a hundred pieces in one hour! The ladies enjoyed the shows and always asked many questions about fashions. If I knew the answer, I would share. If asked something I didn't know, you can be sure I had the answer to that question before the next show.

One example of a question (unrelated to clothing) was asked: "*Why do we set a table the way we do?*" I found the answer while reading about colonial towns *before* we became the country called America. When we arrived in the "new world," we (especially women) tried to be as civil as possible in an uncivilized world. Women began with the dinner table, setting the silverware. The knife blade turned next to the plate was telling a visitor they had enough food to feed them if they wanted to stay and eat. If there wasn't enough food to feed them, the blade of the knife would be turned out from the plate. This would mean no food. From that time on, dinner tables in the United States of America have always been set with the blades of knives turned in, toward the plate. With enough food to eat, all are welcome. We are an abundant nation.

The fashions and artifacts I showed dated from the 1790s to the 1960s. My collection was so large it outgrew my shed and overflowed my home. I owned over two thousand authentic costumes, eight hundred pieces of jewelry and hairpieces, and approximately two hundred fifty pairs of shoes. The ladies enjoyed the high tea and fashion shows. Some of the ladies I met stayed friends with me. Some over thirty years.

At one of the fashion shows, a man came up to me and told me about a movie they were filming on the Olympic Peninsula and asked if I would do the costumes for it. There was an offer of good money for my services, so I said "*Yes.*" When I put a fashion show and tea for a church or other good cause, there was always a great joy and happiness in planning and doing the project. Oh, but this was very different. I was making costumes for a movie. I had no joy working for this or any other movie company. Most people who are actors in the film world are full of themselves. They only want to learn their lines and give no thought to anyone else. I worked on two movies and was paid well. The money did help my household and paid the bills for which I was very thankful for. It was a way of life God gave me for a season.

One of the actors told me, "A person must be a good liar in order to be a good actor because you have to make everyone believe you *are* that person in the movie." Working with film people was hard, but I did plant seeds of the Word of Christ in some of the people. I pray that God, with the Holy Spirit, will grow the seeds to bring forth their salvation. I was talking to people I would never see again. Every now and then I was able to talk to one of them about Christ and tell them He loves us and died for us. James 3:17 says, *"But the wisdom that is from above is first pure, then peaceable, gentle, easy to be intreated (reasonable), full of mercy and good fruits, without partiality and without hypocrisy."* As Christians, we need to always be real and stand in the ways of God's Word with all honesty to each other. Always letting the light of God show around and through us so that we might win others to Christ.

Finding Christ

Jesus said in John 8:31–32, *"If you continue in My word...you are My disciples indeed. And you shall know the truth and the truth will set you free."*

I have seen people ask God to come into their heart, but their lifestyle hasn't changed. Christ says abide in Him and you will be His and you will desire to stay in Him (John 3:67). Jesus Himself said,

> *Except a man be born of water and the spirit, he cannot enter into the Kingdom of God. That which is born of the flesh is flesh and that which is born of the spirit is spirit. Marvel not that I said unto you, you must be born again.*

Christ Himself said this. We must go after Christ with all of our heart. We must live His way and put our wants and lusts behind us. As we grow, we will be a witness for Him. Our hunger will grow, and God will give us a new life in Him, leaving the old life behind us. That *is* being born again in God's Spirit.

"For everyone that doeth evil hateth the light, neither cometh to the light, least his deeds should be reproved" (John 3:20).

Once we truly know the Lord, we have all new desires. That's what being born again is all about. He (God) must increase, but you must decrease.

I pray like Ephesians 1:18 says: *"The eyes of your understanding being enlightened that ye may know what is the hope of His calling and what the riches of the glory of His inheritance in the saints."* Amen!

Remember, *"For by grace are you saved through faith, and that not of yourself, it is a gift of God. Not of works lest any man should boast"* (Ephesians 2:8). God wants us to walk in Him as Christians now that we are His. Our souls and minds are what we give to God or we walk in the flesh. Don't give in to the ways of your flesh of old. You are in Christ now, so walk in Him. It is with our mind we make choices. Read your Bible and learn from it. Right choices will take you to heaven and not to hell. We each make our own choices.

We are now a child of the king in heaven, who is our Lord Jesus Christ. Faith is acting on what the Word says. Go tell somebody about your salvation. When the physical body is dead, and you are in the grave, your spiritual man will live on forever with God. For people who do not know God, Hell awaits them.

Worldly things we see every day, such as on TV and in movies try to normalize sin. Programs like *Ghostbusters* and series like *Casper* have us watching evil spirits, people killing people, homosexuality, and a myriad of other evils. Actually, those two movie examples of spirits are tame compared to what is now pictured on screens. Much of today's film world is demonic and beyond. People do not understand the true nature and danger of those movies. Many TV shows and movies work at normalizing sin and evil in our mind as they actually *try* to draw us into that dark, evil world. In truth, *they are an evil entrapment for unsuspecting minds and hearts.* Consider the rampant, out of control, child molestation and sex trafficking. Consider the hundreds, no thousands, of children that go missing everyday across the world. Connect the dots. Be afraid. Be very afraid. And then run to salvation! For increasingly we are becoming desensitized to biblical warnings! We are being programmed by demonic forces to think good is evil and evil is good! People's minds seem to be fascinated by the sins that fill our world and our cellular screens. A huge push for Christian movies and content is beginning to be felt across the globe. We know this because censorship of our freedom of speech is being openly attacked on a daily basis. Doubt not, it *is* spiritual warfare we are up to our eyeballs in!

We need to learn to walk in the power and anointing of the Holy Spirit. Our God is a God of power and might! As we learn to walk in His very presence, we will be able to move mountains when we pray. Luke 17:6 says:

If ye had faith as a grain of mustard seed, ye might say unto this sycamine tree, Be thou plucked up by the root, and be thou planted in the sea; and it should obey you.

Darkness is growing all around us in spiritual conflict. The darkest of evil has immediate access to everyone, and especially vulnerable are the children. It is as close as the cellular phone in our hand! Even ads that pop up can be very dark. We must be vigilant as to what our children and grandchildren are exposed to! It is vital for us to learn to walk in the power and anointing of God's Holy Spirit. The church needs to raise up in prayer. Christ has already won the victory. That victory was paid for by His blood. Let all of us, as Christians, fight the good fight for God. *We must spread the good news!* Our win should be for Christ. Do battle in prayer to heaven for lost souls around the world. Stand in prayer against establishments that put out the sinful movies, for they *are* normalizing our minds and the minds of children with their films of sin, despair, and darkness. Pray, pray, pray. Help people become aware of the TV and films filling minds with corrupt garbage that people are watching. Pray fervently for more good quality Christian films. The corrupt film industry is desperate to shut down independent Christian films that are growing daily. Truly, it is a battle for our minds and our hearts. We cannot be mediocre about our everyday life anymore. We must fight the good fight—and that *is* the battle of good and evil. Know ye not it is *all* scriptural? Again I give you Ephesians 6:10–13+. The full armor of God!

Growing up in the 1940s and 1950s was such a good time for families. We were outside playing and doing healthy things. On Sundays, most families were seen going to church together. Families sat down together at the dinner table and talked with each other. Evenings were spent listening to radio programs or outside playing. Now individuals watch TV or cellphone screens night and day. Most of the time, children are watching their choice of TV or other cellular shows by themselves, rarely conversing with other family members. We as Christians must help the next generations make right choices regarding what they should watch until they are old enough to make their own. We live and die with our choices in life. God gave us a free will. The power to choose is ours.

Desire of the Spirit

As I sit here writing my story of life, love, joy, hope, suffering, fear, and dying three times, I realize I'm submitting my life for all to read. I truly hope people will learn about God and prayer. I hope someone will learn we can go through it all and come out the other side with peace, if not joy. I have written about my life and most of my choices, the good and the bad. All of my life I've jumped right into every situation! Both feet, eyes wide open, and with my whole heart. Always believing God was with me and knowing that in boldness, there is freedom. I believe right from the start God called me to win souls and for the working of His calling. All three of my husbands have passed away. Years have flown by and still I pray for God to use me, even in my old age. Once again I have a spiritual fire burning inside of me. With every day that passes, I find God using me in different ways and am enjoying His work with a deeper joy and love. I have an understanding I did not have when I was younger and the spiritual freedom knowing when I die, I'm alright. If I stay on earth longer, I'm alright. So whether I stay or go, I'm fine. Christ is my Lord. My desire is to do His will in my walk on earth for the rest of my life (Philippians 1:20–21)!

 I know people who think they're right with God, but their words and what they say and do does not line up with God's Word. The Bible tells us to search the scriptures for in them are they which testify of Him. Some people think they are saved and fine with God. However, what comes out of their mouths are filthy words. That kind of life does not line up with God's Word. After being around them just a few minutes, you know something is very wrong. I find myself praying right then and there in the Spirit, so they will repent. Our thoughts must be clean also.

God has provided His Word, so we can go to Him and ask Him to save us. He will manifest Himself to you. After getting saved, He will give you an infilling of His Holy Spirit with speaking in tongues. That's a beautiful gift God gives His children once they are saved.

> *And, being assembled together with them, commanded them that they should not depart from Jerusalem, but wait for the promise of the Father, which, saith he, ye have heard of Me. For John truly baptized with water, but you shall be baptized with the Holy Ghost not many days hence.* (Acts 1:4–5)

> *And suddenly there came a sound from Heaven as of a rushing mighty wind, and it filled all the house where they were sitting. And there appeared unto them cloven tongues like as of fire, and it sat on each of them. And they were all filled with the Holy Ghost, and began to speak with other tongues as the Spirit gave them utterance.* (Acts 2:2–4)

That is a wonderful gift directly from God. When the Spirit came on me, I was immediately warm and felt electricity going all through me. That power was incredibly sweet, and I knew it was God.

That gift is for all Christians. However, the devil will battle with your mind for you. He does not want you to get this gift because power comes with this. You will be a Light for Christ wherever you go. In Acts 3:6–8, Peter took his authority and said,

> *Silver and gold, I have none, but such as I have I give to you. In the name of Jesus Christ of Nazareth rise up and walk. And he (Peter) took him (the lame man) by the right hand, and lifted him up and immediately his feet and ankle bones received strength and he, leaping up, stood and walked and*

entered with them into the temple, walking and leaping and praising God.

God's healing power has been generated and is now deposited inside of every born-again, spirit-filled, tongue-talking believer. God fills you to be His hands on earth. Tell the world what God has done for you. Be a light for everyone. If you're a Christian, you must set aside worldly things be "sold out" to Christ by mouth, word, and deed. None of us can out give God! The more you give of yourself for Him, the more He gives back with love and mercy to you. If you want the lights to come on, don't call the power company. You must flip the light switch on. (In the same way, you have to flip the switch to generate the power as a Christian.) That is, if you are a believer now, and I pray you are!

God has already done His part. He raised Jesus from the dead and left us to use His authority and heal the sick (Matthew 10:5–8). *"Freely you have received, freely give."* We are saved by grace. God is with us always to the end. Jesus now has given us His authority and His spiritual law. We can enforce this law by the power of the Holy Spirit now living within. That means God has told us to *command the works of His hands,* which is everything He has already provided in Christ. We have made a contract with God under His command. Go into the world and preach the gospel to everyone who will listen. Minister about Christ and His saving power to other people. Release God's power, in His name, for God's saving grace to the world. The Lord will open unto you His good treasure. Heaven will give rain unto your land in His season, and bless all the work of your hands. He has called us for this.

The Holy Spirit

The mission of the world awaits all of us as Christians. We must be God's hands. I can't imagine why God keeps giving us more of something if He knows we're not going to use what He has given us already. Can you? No Christian is going to know the fullness of the Holy Spirit unless we are obedient to Him in all the realms of witnessing to others. We have access to the Holy Spirit now. The greatest event of the church since Christ left earth. It is for all of us as a "born-again child of God." The Book of Acts is full of His giving of the Spirit. Love, power, joy, and victory are all in Him. "But you will receive power when the Holy Spirit has come upon you and you shall be My witnesses" (Acts 1:8). You must get this: it says "witnesses." There is not one person claiming to be a child of Christ that cannot speak to anyone what Christ has done for them. We must share Jesus with others and the relevance that He has to change lives. It was in the Book of Acts that God gave us His Holy Spirit on the day of Pentecost. Jesus's mother was there with the one hundred and twenty people and all who were present received Him (Acts 2)! It is a celebration of a wonderful gift God gave and is still giving to all believers today. Just ask for it. Open your mouth and start praising Jesus and loving him. *You must be speaking to receive it.* Give Him your voice. His children need to know the abundance through this experience. Then go into the world and preach the gospel to everyone in your corner of the world (Mark 16:15). God Himself will anoint and equip you as you speak to each person. Go and joyously tell someone!

A Prophetic Word

In 2000, my friend Nina received a prophetic word. This is for all that have a heart for God, and I am going to share it with you now.

I want you completely saturated with the Word—I do not want one word spoken that is not of me (not mine). Memorize my Word for it will be the wellspring you will rely upon in the work which lies ahead for you. I have heard your cries for more of me, and it pleases me. Just know your time is very close now; I will use you mightily. But now my child, you must be serious, even zealous about this saturation. See it like a sponge which is set in a bowl of water. It will absorb until every fiber is full. It can only give out that with which it is filled. There are unsubmitted and undisciplined areas in your life which are keeping you from moving forward. They will cause stagnation if left within the sponge like bacteria tainting even souring the pure water. Do not fill your sponge with worldly things, even as innocent as they seem to you. You must fill up to overflowing with me, so that anything that flows back out is of me. I have told you that there are some things which are not to be spoken out but will be completely saturated the Word—I do not want one word spoken that is not of me (not mine). Memorize my Word for it will be the wellspring you will rely upon in the work which lies ahead for you. I have heard your cries for more of me, and it pleases me. Just know your time is very close now; I will use you mightily.

I think this would be a prayer of our hearts that God would answer *if* we could give God everything, every area of our lives. God's true desire is only to want each of us to be all that we can be our very best in Him.

Paint...A Gift from God

It was April of 2007. My home was an ugly color and really needed to be painted. Driving east on Highway 101 in Port Angeles one evening, an amazing thing happened. Near the Mount Angeles cemetery, two five-gallon containers fell off of a truck right in front of my car. I stopped and checked them out. They were paint containers, and they had not popped, opened, nor been damaged in any way!

A man drove up right then, stopped, and offered to load them into my car. He did, and I drove as fast as I could to catch up with the truck, but it disappeared out of sight. I ended up taking both containers home. They were the perfect colors for my house. One was off-white which I could use on the entire house. The other was a dark beige and enough for the trim. That was a real blessing!

The miracle gift of paint did not stop there! My son David had a friend named Chuck who needed a place to stay for two weeks. In exchange for rent, Chuck stayed in my home, used those two buckets of paint, and painted the whole house! I was very happy and very blessed! God not only supplied paint in colors I wanted, He also blessed me with someone willing and able! Chuck did an excellent job, and my house still looks great! That ten gallons of paint dropping off of a truck right in front of my car was a miracle. God made it possible for me to have the paint I needed to improve my house. Could the man who offered to put it into my car have been one of God's holy angels? I believe he was indeed an angel. I believe God's hand was on the entire project as I received yet another blessing.

THROUGH DARK CLOUDS SHINES HOLY LIGHT!

After Chuck finished painting everything, he decided to stay an extra week. As a bonus for me allowing him to stay, he boarded up the crawl space under my house so animals could not get in. Thank you, Lord God, for every single one of those special blessings! Thank you!

Fear

When things come up in our lives that bring fear, *know this.* There is no fear with Christ. If we ask Him for bread, He will not give us a stone. He is love and that is never ending. For God loved the world and gave us his son, Jesus, so we can come back to Him, receive forgiveness, and *know* that all of this is in our hearts. Every one that does evil hates the light and does not come to the light, lest his deeds should be reproved. But he that does truth comes to the light so His deeds may be made manifest and are wrought in God (paraphrased).

Here is a good thing to remember about "fear":

F = False
E = Evidence
A = Appearing
R = Real

Fear is not God's will. That word comes from the devil. He will use our mind to keep us down, to feel beaten and defeated. God gives us the power to resist the devil. When *in knowing*, we say: "*In Jesus's name, leave!*" the devil *must* leave. The devil is a bully, and he'll keep coming back to our mind and fight to get a hold of you by harassment. *Sincere prayer overcomes fear every time.* God has given us power and authority over the devil. Rebuke the devil, and he will flee from you. That is God's Word. Resist means "to actively fight against." Resistance is active.

God gave us power and authority over *all* devils and *all* means *all* (James 4:7). Submit yourselves therefore to God. Resist the devil, and he will flee from you. The truth concerning authority will work when you submit to God and are seeking Him with your whole heart. When you are submitted to God, you can resist the devil. You will have the power. God wants *all* to be saved. Each person must believe on the Lord Jesus Christ to receive salvation for themselves. God gave each of us responsibility for our own choices. That is our free will.

"*Believe on the Lord Jesus Christ, and thou shalt be saved, and thy house*" (Acts 16:31). God leaves it up to us to choose the way we will go. Our minds are what we choose with. God gave us that when He made Adam and Eve and gave them the opportunity to choose!

> *Enter ye in at the straight gate. For wide is the gate and broad is the way that leadeth to destruction, and many there be that go in there. Because strait is the gate and narrow is the way which leadeth unto life and few there be that find it.* (Matthew 7:13)

Every single person has a choice. If you choose God, I will see you "up there," "down here" or "in the air!"

Mother told me a story about her great grandmother, and she was not sure about her salvation. She knew the Bible story of *"One shall be taken, and the other left. Watch therefore for ye know not what hour your Lord doth come."* Her husband owned a grain mill, and she would not walk with her husband to the mill. She was afraid she would be the one left behind while her husband would be taken! I think my great-great-grandmother had no faith and didn't know what grace was. It is God's grace that saves us. It is not by works and is a free gift from God. Ephesians 2–8 says: "*It is by grace we are saved through faith. This is not of our doing but a gift of God.*" We no longer need to suffer punishment of sin.

Reflecting on Spiritual Warfare

In life, I've found out it's not easy for people to serve God and be sold out to the Lord. They're willing to talk to you about God, but before you leave them, you know they really don't know God in their heart. They start defending their point of view until Hades freezes over then skate on the ice. You don't get anywhere with people who talk and defend themselves in that way. However, the Spirit of God is always working. Sooner or later they think over what you told them and hopefully yield to God's will.

God wants people to completely surrender their life over to Him. This is the cost of being His disciple. Complete surrender. Christ purchased us through His blood and set us free from our troubled conscience. Salvation is ours because of Jesus brought life and light to our souls where there was only darkness. Jesus won our freedom from *all* sins through His death and resurrection. He sacrificed His life so we might be saved. Through Him, we have gained the kingdom of heaven. Reading the Word of God every day will help us grow and give us a passion to believe truth and become a disciple of Christ. When we go to war, we battle against our enemy with all understanding of the relationship we are going into. Our goal is to overcome the enemy. We no longer worry about conflict with victory as a Christian. We win over sin because it is now no longer the issue. The price has been paid by Jesus. He overcame sin so that He could offer mercy for all sins, that we might receive salvation. Jesus did this nearly two thousand years ago. He died on the cross for *all*. Reading the Word of God will help our walk and promote spiritual growth. Now we can have the experience of victory over conflict with the enemy. The enemy gets your cooperation through your mind, through deception. This is war and exposes the enemy for what he is. Our mind is where the battle starts and where we make all of our choices. The conflict of good and evil lies within every choice we make. Our mind declares and equips us with good weapons from the Word of God and clears our flesh of all undesirable desires within.

We must declare the Word when temptation comes. The Bible says in 1 Corinthians 10:13:

> *There hath no temptations taken you but such as is common to man, but God is faithful, who will not suffer (permit) you to be tempted above that ye are able but will with the temptation also make a way to escape that ye may be able to bear it.*

The Word tells us we can stand fast in obedience to God. *"Nevertheless he that standeth steadfast in his heart having no necessity, but hath power over his own will and hath so decreed in his heart"* (Corinthians 7:37).

We are overcomers with God's Word only. The enemy is always battling us in our minds to give us conflict and deception to get us to sin. But there is peace in God and we need to look to Him for all of our answers.

> *Know ye not that the unrighteous shall not inherit the kingdom of God.?"* (1 Corinthians 6:9)

> *Flee fornication. Every sin a man doeth is without the body: but he that committeth fornication sinneth against his own body. What? Know ye not that your body is the temple of the Holy Ghost which is in you, which ye have of God, and ye are not your own? (1 Corinthians 18–19)*

We are flesh, and we like doing and feeding the flesh in all we enjoy that brings pleasure to us, but there is a price to pay—the guilt of sin. The Word of God is a weapon we can use in battle and in our darkest hours. We speak the Word aloud and can win the battle that is in our mind! We are more than conquerors through Jesus Christ!

My Sister Cotha

"The Lord is not slack concerning His promise, as some men count slackness; but is longsuffering to us-ward, not willing that any should perish, but that all should come to repentance" (2 Peter 3:9).

I stood looking into Cotha's face and remembering her being a second mother to me when I was young. My older sisters, Cotha, Margaret, and Wylo Dean, would take my twin sister Ann, and I with them everywhere—on dates with their boyfriends, to church, and all the different places they went. Mother wasn't able to care for us because she was sick after we were born.

Cotha was always with us. Even when she was married, she still seemed to be around. After her husband died, she moved close to Mother and Dad with her only son, Bill Jr. She taught us to dance and helped us learn what work was all about. When Ann and I would go with her, people would say, "Oh how nice! Mother and daughters are out together!"

Cotha would say, *"No, just sisters out for the evening."*

Growing up around her, we began picking up her habits, such as smoking and trying to act like her, never giving a thought to Christ.

Soon, we were going to night clubs, N.C.O. clubs, dancing, smoking, and doing the things we saw her do. My older sisters grew up in the depression years and didn't always have what we younger sisters had, which was a better, more prosperous lifestyle in childhood. When I was grown and married and started having children, Cotha was always there, helping with my children. I was glad because

I was only eighteen years old in 1957 when I had my first child and my husband, LeRoy, was always out of town. My life was raising my children. Cotha had a big, loving heart but was not living a Christ-centered life. About that time, my husband started his own business, Mills and Davis.

In 2012, Cotha became very sick with Alzheimer's, like my mother-in-law I had taken care of years ago. However, Cotha was a different type of person and had grown up in a home that believed in God. She also had cancer in her whole body with only a short time to live. My sister had always been there for me, and now it was my time to take care of her. In addition, her son Bill would be there anytime we needed him. Hospice care began coming every other day. What a difference taking care of her than when I took care of my mother-in-law!

Cotha was into religion, praying to other saints and not to Christ. I would say, "Sister, Jesus is the way to God, not Mary and other saints. He is the only one that said I am the way, the truth, and the life, no one comes to the Father, but by me." As my sister lay there, I would tell her, "Sister, you can't get to heaven by those saints! The Bible says to be renewed in the spirit of your mind and put on the new man, which after God, is created in righteousness and true holiness! We must think spiritual songs and sing and make melodies in our hearts to the Lord."

Many times Cotha and I sang the old songs we both knew. Every day she sang, "Do Lord, oh do Lord." Sometimes she would call out, "Sister! Come sing with me!" Her mind would go to our older sisters, growing up in the south when they were invited to sing together in churches. They loved to sing! It didn't matter which church they sang in as they sang in many different ones!

Cotha was into religion, praying to other saints and not to Christ, so I always told her, "Sister, Jesus is the way to God, not Mary and other saints." My sister was religious, but as the Alzheimer's progressed, I watched her mind growing closer and closer to Christ. Cotha began talking to Him daily. Her son, Bill, put her in a rest home, and we often drove down to see her. As soon as we arrived, we could hear her singing old southern songs all the way down the hall!

The caregivers would be singing right along with her! That was pure joy for Bill and me.

In John 10:9, Christ said, "I *am the Door, by Me if any man enter in, he shall be saved, and shall go in and out, and find pastures.*" When my sister Cotha died, she had Jesus in her heart. I believe she is walking on the streets of gold with my parents and all the other family members who are in heaven.

Cotha had been in my life, teaching me much over the years. Being with her in her last days was all in God's plan. Looking back on my mother, daddy, sisters, and my life, I know God's plan was there. Even when I was a little girl, God had been waiting for me to say "Yes" so He could bring His plans into my life. Thank you, Jesus, for being there in *all* things. God's love is never ending.

God grant unto thy servants that with all boldness I may speak Your Word by the name of your holy son, Jesus. Thank you Lord. Amen.

Freedom

I have become a disciple. Being a disciple is being the Word of Christ (Romans 10:17, John 1:12–13, John 15:16). *"And God said, Let there be light: and there was light"* (*Genesis 1:3*). I am wrapped up into the kingdom through the Word of God. It's cutting through the darkness of my soul and my heart, bringing life and light. Just as it did on that first day!

It is the same word that became flesh and dwelt among us. Christ Jesus won our freedom from sin and death, through His death and resurrection. He is the one who found the treasure hidden in the field and then gave all he had to purchase it. He is the one who paid the pearl of great price and sacrificed His *all*. We are the treasure (recipients). The kingdom of God is seen and experienced only through the reign of Jesus who died for the ungodly. For *all* are born into sin.

"For when we were yet without strength, in due time Christ died for the ungodly" (Romans 5:6). He gave his blood for mankind and brought light and life where only death and darkness reigned before. *Because of His sacrifice, He purchased us through His blood.* We can now possess freedom from condemnation and death. Salvation is ours because of what Christ has done. It has been freely given to *all*, with His Son's blood and resurrection. It is the freedom of our soul and conscience we so desperately need and long for. Let us share the living Word. Because of it, we can rejoice in it. Amen.

"And the Word was made flesh, and dwelt among us, (and we beheld his glory, the glory as of the only begotten of the Father), full of grace and truth" (John 1:14).

Here is the sinner's prayer: *"Lord, I believe you died for me. Come into my heart and forgive me of my sins. Help me to be a child of yours and follow your word in Jesus' name. Amen."* Now, you are a true believer. Begin first by reading the Bible. Start with the New Testament and read every day. Study until you remember the Word and then do what it says.

Paul wrote letters to the churches he had established to encourage learning and growth. Christians are to be concerned and encourage other believers to help them grow in faith. Our highest priority should be doing God's Work. Always. Wrong conduct and speech only hinders His work. Our light will not shine as it should if we live for ourselves with harmful habits needing to be broken. Focus should always be on living a Christian life that is good. Every day we as Christians need to delve into the scriptures. The Bible is alive and always relevant. It will help us be the Light God wants us to be for those that do not know Christ as their Savior. God's Word always nourishes His people's spirits and encourages them to live better. The world around us influences our lives every day. This is why we study scripture. Memorizing it helps us stay close to God. Then when we are on a spiritual battlefield, the scriptures we have learned are our weapons.

The Bible tells us in order to live abundantly, we must serve the Lord Jesus Christ who became our example for everything we do in life. We learn prayer is the foundation for trusting the Lord. King David said, *"My hope is in God all the day long."* As Christians, we need to learn to glorify God in our attitudes, even in hard times. In suffering, we need to be patient and praise God for all things, always. Think about this: Christ *never* complained as he went to the cross. He trusted the Father just as we must. In trusting God, we come out of darkness and meet the light! Understanding that the fruit of the Spirit is always in season allows us to begin the greatest adventure of our life and grow in the fullness of Christ.

Omar, a Muslim Man

A friend of mine, John, stopped by my house one Saturday afternoon. He wanted me to talk to a Muslim friend of his with him. Omar (not his real name) was from Iran. John's plan was to ask me to his house for dinner that evening so we could both talk to Omar. John felt that together we might be able to reach him and bring him to Christ. I agreed, so off we went. We were having a nice dinner when John asked Omar, *"Can we talk to you about Christ Jesus"* and I asked, *"Has Allah ever given you a miracle or answered a prayer for you?"*

He said, "No." So I began telling him everything Christ has done for me, including answering many prayers. Omar started asking questions about many things. We couldn't answer all of his questions fast enough, but I told him, *"If you will pray, Omar, and ask Christ to make Himself known to you, He will."* I also said, *"God can give you a dream to show you He is real. Christ took sin on Himself, so we might have salvation and forgiveness, for all that we have done wrong in our lives."*

We had talked for two solid hours when Omar suddenly stood up and said, *"I have to go get some air."* Out the door he went, leaving us at the table. We sat there for thirty minutes before he came back to talk with us again. We told him of the many things Jesus has done for both of us, including healings and miracles done in Jesus's name.

I said, *"Satan wants to control your thoughts and God pulls at our hearts. You know, Omar, Christ Jesus will come right in your bedroom, if you ask him to come into your heart."* We could see spiritual warfare going on inside of him and knew *immediately* Satan's deceptions had already begun in his head! I knew John was making intercession in the Holy Spirit as every now, and then he would say aloud, *"In the name of Jesus!"*

Soon after that, Omar said, *"I have to go to my class at Peninsula College early tomorrow, so I will see you there, John."*

Shortly after that, I went home. That night, John and I prayed for Omar's soul.

The next day, Omar went to John and said he hadn't slept at all that night. He said he knew Jesus Christ was coming into his room and even jammed a chair under the door knob! He said he could only think of what we had told him the evening before. Omar then told John he wanted to do whatever he could to know Jesus and see for himself what we were talking about. Omar received Jesus Christ! We do not know how things turned out because he went back to Iran to be with his family. However, we prayed for all of them to understand about Christ and what Omar had done when he accepted Jesus. He would likely be paying a large price to identify with Christ and to find his place there. As a Muslim in Iran that converted to Christianity, he could be killed. Muslims believe the Lord Jesus is a prophet only. Omar told us that going back to his country was a fearful thing for him. His family were all Muslims. He knew it would be very hard for him to live in Iran again. His life would be on the line daily as his journey to Christianity from Islam would be for the rest of his life. We must pray for all Christians in the Muslim world. They have come to Christ but are living in Muslim countries. Those places are very hostile to the gospel. Their concept of sin is radically different. Many believers pay a price, even death, identifying with Christ Jesus. John and I prayed earnestly for Omar and that he would be fine as a new convert, that he would find the fellowship of Christians for support and spiritual growth, that he would know he needed the encouragement of Christians in Iran. Persecutions of Christians in Iran (and the world) are real, horrific, and happening as I write.

Lord, let this be a prayer for the persecuted church for all who read this. In Jesus's name, Amen.

God answers prayer *anywhere!* When standing on the promises of God, our prayers go throughout the whole world. The Bible teaches us our Father is committed to answering the prayers of His children. God also gave us authority with divinely empowered speech. *Declare that authority and command it in Jesus's name, with life-changing hope in the Gospel around the world.* I have seen this many times as I walked and prayed for many people, here and around the world. Believe God and His Word. There is nothing like going all the way with the ministry of the Lord and His Word. You too can bring life changing help to others where ever they are. When we pray, amazing things can happen.

Hospital Stay Due to Heart Attack

My friend Cookie loves sunflowers. You will find them in her home showing their loveliness. Sunflowers alone are a reason to marvel. A sunflower outside always faces the sun. As they grow, all sunflowers face east in the mornings toward the rising sun. As the sun moves across the sky, their colorful heads follow the sun from east to west throughout the day, facing the sun for nourishment. This is a symbol of why prayer matters. Like the sunflower, we all need sustenance in our prayer life. Our spiritual light only survives and grows with the light. Without the "Son," we wither and die, just as the beautiful sunflower would without its light from the sun.

Prayer is the soul of Christianity. My friends, Cookie and Nina, came every day when I was in the hospital. I was there a month, but in that time, I died three times. I was on life support for two and a half weeks, but they came every day to be with me and pray. Nina would come in, hold my hand, and pray. Later, Cookie would come in and pray. My son, David was there the first nine days and saw Cookie coming and going. He knew she came to the hospital every day to see me.

Doug, a friend of David's, came by and insisted David go home to get clean clothes and eat a meal. David went home and not only freshened up, he got on Facebook. People all over the world began praying for me. We know now over four hundred people were praying. David knew prayer was the answer because he had won a second battle for his life. The second time was with cancer when he was only twenty-eight years old. He is now sixty and still cancer free. Praise God!

Day after day, Nina and Cookie came by and prayed faithfully and daily, along with my David.

I lay for two and a half weeks on life support. Every day the hospital staff asked my son to unplug the life support. David always said, *"No, wait."* On a Thursday morning, he was thinking he should let me go. That day, Cookie had been there praying and was about to leave. However, she looked up and saw Nina coming in. That was the first time both of them were together with me at the same time.

Here were three people, praying every day for me. Not together nor at the same time, but always praying. This particular day, my son David had decided to let the doctors unplug the life support systems and let me go to be with the Lord. As God would have it, all three of my strongest prayer warriors were there together!

Nina stood and talked a while with David in the hallway, *and said "Let me pray first before you unplug her."* Nina began praying in earnest. A moment later she said, *"Hey! Her cheek just moved!"* The nurse said I had been on life support for such a long time, it was just a muscle moving. Nina said, *"No!"*

David stepped over to the hospital bed and slapped the headboard hard, making a really loud sound! When he did that, my eyelids flew open! He yelled, *"Hallelujah!"* A hallelujah chorus then broke loose throughout the floor of the hospital! We live in a small town and knew many of the nurses as friends. David told me later a lot of people we didn't even know came in and rejoiced with us! Small-town "community" at its best!

God answered prayers, their prayers. I was being called a miracle woman. I was dead, but now I'm alive! After all that time on life support, I was now alive and awake again! Praise God!

At first, I had no idea of anything that was happening. I did not know I had even died nor understood I had been on life support. I knew people around me were helping me. People would come in and ask me what day is it, etc. I didn't care, I just wanted to rest. As days went on, I became more aware. I couldn't move my left side and couldn't seem to put things together in my head. However, I slowly began to know and recognize people as they came in to see me.

May 7, 2015, I was having trouble with my heart and had gone to Seattle for a checkup. Doctors said I had something called "ablation for atrial fibrillation of the heart." They did a procedure called "heart oblation." I stayed overnight but went home the next day. I was feeling good and looking forward to doing what I had been doing the past five years, volunteering for the food bank. I had also been going with Pastor Thomas every weekend to feed the homeless, at the city pier. However, that wasn't to be.

Once more God had plans for me I did not know. He wasn't done with me yet. Not knowing what to do with my time, I decided to wait upon the Lord while I was to spend a few days resting.

Sometimes in life we ask the question, *"Why am I here?"* We all need know there is a purpose for our life. This is where the truth of God comes in. We are all searching for our purpose. We need to look to our Creator and wait for what God is trying to teach us and why we exist. The doors will open for us as we walk in and out of them.

For some time, I had invited several homeless ladies to live with me. They were a pleasure to have, and we truly enjoyed each other. Later, as I healed from my heart attack, they were a great help in care for my healing.

I went into the OM Hospital the ninth of May and was discharged on July 31, 2015.

Before I had gone into the hospital, I had been having signs and symptoms of pneumonia but didn't know it. I was getting ready to go to church when my son came over. He said, *"Mother, I called 911 because you're not right with the shortness of breath, so you're going to the hospital."* That's how I came to be in the hospital.

After I left the house in the ambulance, David followed in his car. I arrived at the hospital and was rushed into the ER. They immediately began taking my vitals and decided I needed treatment. They were hooking me up to an IV when David (still driving to the hospital) called me on my cell phone and asked how I was doing. I did not remember anything or even the conversation. David told me later the very last thing I said to him was, *"Oh, honey, something's wrong, my heart is pounding!"* Then David heard utter chaos and nurses yelling, *"Code blue! Code blue!"* Can you imagine your son hearing that as he's driving, trying to get to his mother as quickly as humanly possible? David arrived to find them trying to revive me the first time! What a horrible experience for him to have gone through!

Doctor Swan was the ER doctor that took care of me. The last thing my son said to me as I left home in the ambulance was *"Don't let them give you anything that stimulates your heart, Mother."* Doctor Swan in ER gave me Losyn because he suspected I had pneumonia. *He also knew I had the heart oblation just two days before!* As soon as the Losyn was put into my IV tube, I *died.*

Two friends of mine were working in the hospital that afternoon. An RN named Vashina and my pastor's wife, Rita. God's hand was already on me. Those two are incredible prayer warriors and were "on the job" immediately! Dr. Swan began to work on me. He worked for two hours before I was put on life support in ICU, also giving me antibiotics to treat the aspiration pneumonia.

In ICU, I began having cardiac arrest again and was shocked out of ventricular fibrillation. I developed a torsade pattern and was shocked out of that. When they transferred me to the critical care unit, I went into full PEA cardiac arrest! I died three times. However, God did not allow me to stay dead. My pastor, Pastor Omer Vigoren, told me later, *"God is not done with you yet, Nan. God has something He still wants you to do."*

Later I went to my doctor and got a written paper on my condition that said: *The patient has really made a very dramatic recovery and reporting improvement after a very rocky and prolonged course in the hospital.* The hospital report I also got stated: *The patient stabilized on the ventilator albeit with pulmonary infiltrators and continued antibiotics. Also noted left side weakness and a small left pneumothorax on chest x-rays.*

The chaos and lots of physical stuff that transpired was, of course, not written down. They had broken nine of my ribs. In spite of that and with all of their work, they had kept me alive! My left side had paralysis, and I was having a hard time with my left hand. When they had worked on me, I knew nothing. However, at the beginning of all this, as I watched the nurse putting the Losyn into my IV, I *knew* I was going to die. After that, I knew nothing at all. However,

I felt a peace I had never felt before. It was such a sweet peace that I gave into it and went to sleep. I knew nothing until thirty days later.

Somehow, I did see God's hand as I slept. One time I remember seeing the sky. Looking over the horizon with water below, in a silhouette of black and white, I saw the head of a lady I knew. It was my friend Nina Fisher. She had her hand on my hand as I was laying on the bed. Nina was praying for me. Somewhere else, I knew my friend Cookie Allison was also praying for me. I knew who they were. God spoke to me and said, *"Prayer has brought you back!"* I know prayer is for reaching up to God, for His will to be done. God did a miracle in me, for *His* Glory! I thank God for David, Nina, Cookie, my church, and all who prayed fervently for me. I cannot thank them enough. Thank you, God.

I know even Christ prayed on the day He knew He was going to die and His Father heard Him.

My son, David, had posted my medical needs on his Facebook page (over four hundred are on it). Prayers began going up all over the world! I am still receiving cards from people who continue to pray for me! Thank you, my David!

While I was in recovery at the rest home, October 4, 2015, I heard the Lord speak to me. He said, *"I raised Lazarus once, but I have raised you three times for the glory of God. This sickness is not unto death but that My Son Jesus will be glorified." Wow!* Since the Lord restored my life, I've been in many waiting rooms of doctors' offices or in waiting rooms for medical tests. Many times I've had the opportunity to talk to people about Jesus. It is one of the ways God is still using me to glorify His son, Jesus. For me, this sickness was not unto lasting death. Yet, only prayer brought me back. *This I know.*

God has always had his hand on my life, always waiting for me to come to Him in all that I do.

David's Childhood Accident Consequence

Now that David is a grow man, evidence of his childhood accident is still with him. He still has metal in his skull and also has "tics" in his speech. Sometimes, he makes a click or little grunting sound in a sentence. Sometimes a word does not come out right, either slurred or mispronounced. Even so, God has blessed him in many ways. David has much compassion, many talents. He's a hard worker, has a good sense of humor, and has a great talent working with his hands.

David also has narcolepsy, a sleeping disorder where he suddenly falls asleep for a few minutes. While this is happening, he moves in very slow motion with his eyes wide open, but he is sleeping. You would never know he's suddenly asleep, but his mind goes blank. He does not hear nor respond to anything a person says to him while in this sudden sleep state. When he wakes up a few minutes or an hour later, he does not know anything that was said to him while he was "out"!

God has been very good to David over the years. First, sparing his life when he was three years old and again, later in life, when he was twenty-eight, he had cancer. After several very rough years of treatments and remission, he developed cancer again. However, God answered many prayers and spared David's life once more.

During my illness with the heart condition in 2015, David stayed at the hospital with me nine days before a friend came and took him home to eat and clean up. While I was in the hospital, David brought me flowers, but I was so ill at the time I did not even know it. The card that came with the flowers had a printed message: "When life gives you lemons, make cocktails." The handwritten note David added to this card said: *I could have never been blessed with a greater mom than you. I thank God for the Greatest Gift ever in my life. We love you, Mom—(signed) David and the Kids!*

David is a good son! He lives next door, does all of my yard work, and anything else I need—like shopping and paying bills when I'm unable to do it myself. He has adopted a boy, Skylar, and is a wonderful single father to him. They're a great team!

Medicine for Life

Our life moves in the direction of our dominant thoughts (Proverbs 23:7).

We will reap emotions based on what we focus our attention on (Romans 8:6).

We need to learn to keep our thoughts on God and His Word (Isaiah 26:3).

Our emotions will follow based on what we think. God tells us in the Word that we must think on the right things to receive the right results.

When we keep our minds stayed upon the Lord, the peace of God will keep our heart and mind (Philippians 4:8).

God made us so that our physical body and emotional health follow the way that we think. God's Word is life unto us that find it, and His Word brings health through the way we learn to think, believe, and do what the Biblical Word tells us. The Bible says He sent His Word and healed them. We need to take daily doses of reading His Word as medicine so that we can live right.

God will never take control over our life without our consent and agreement. He wants to work with us in daily life. When we take in God's Word by reading and being obedient, we are putting the Word inside of us and allowing the power of faith to work in and for us. Then God's power is released into our lives. Our mind needs to be filled with God's Word. His power then works in a way that is in direct proportion to how we believe. Then we will see God's mighty works in our lives.

John 8:32 says it is the truth that sets people free.

God does not want us to be double minded and will not violate the free will He has given to us. Jesus wants to do His work in each person—in *all* of us. However, He will not do anything in us until we invite Him to come in to our hearts or sincerely ask Him to help us with an issue or situation.

The Bible tells us in Mark 6:5:

> Jesus went to His own home town and could not do any mighty works there. Jesus said to them, *"A prophet is not without honor, but in his own country, and among his own kin, and in his own house. He (Jesus) could do not mighty work there, save (except) He lay His Hands upon a few sick folk and healed them."*

Most chose not to believe in Him. God is a gentleman. He will never push Himself upon any person who does not want Him. He honors the free will (choice) He alone gave us. Jesus stands at the door of our hearts and knocks. He calls for us to let Him come in. Each person has to choose to open the door and invite Him to come in. If we receive Him into our hearts and ask Him to forgive our sins (all things we have done wrong), then He will come in. If we harden our hearts and refuse to invite Jesus in, that is called unbelief. That unbelief prevents God from moving in our lives here on earth and separates us from God. Unbelief condemns a person to burn for all eternity unless they repent and accept Jesus at some point in their lifetime. This is a serious warning. God will not move in our life without our invitation and cooperation. God will not force us to accept Jesus. For those who do accept Jesus, there is an abundance of blessings that becomes available to us in this life. Then when we die, we gain heaven with all of the beauty, rewards, and blessings for all of eternity.

Proverbs 23:7, the Word of God tells us "as a man (any person) thinks in his heart, so is he. Eat and drink, saith he (a person) to thee, but his heart is not with you." (There is no true fellowship). Romans

8:6 tells us God wants us not to be carnally-minded—following sinful thoughts and choices—for that leads to death. "Grace and peace be multiplied unto you through the knowledge of God, and of Jesus our Lord" (2 Peter 1:2).

Loretta Anne, a Roommate

Loretta, a sixty-two-year-old lady, has rented a bedroom at the other end of my home for almost two years. She moved across country in a bus, from the cold state of Minnesota to Washington State. Loretta gave up everything she had to move here. She had a job before she moved in with me but needed a car to get to work. A few weeks after she moved in, she was able to buy a car. Now she is able to drive the fifteen miles to and from her job in Sequim, Washington.

Loretta is a believer who will stop me when I speak a negative thought. She tells me, "*Stop! Reject that kind of thinking!*" Our attitude can get us into trouble.

I would say, "*Yes, my friend, thank you, I know better.*" So now I say for all of us "to go to God." Build on God's Word. The negative we think and speak keeps us in the wilderness. Talk to God in prayer. God can and will give you a change of heart. God wants to bless us beyond our wildest imagination! We make mistakes, but God will forgive us and restore us to His holiness. He is faithful and just to forgive us and cleanses us from all unrighteousness.

The more we read the Bible, the more our faith grows. The Scripture is given by inspiration from God. All Scripture is "*profitable for doctrine, for reproof, for correction, for instruction in righteousness*" (2 Timothy 3:16). We will learn the awesome wonder of God with His Word. The Holy Spirit will speak to us as we read the Scripture and will quicken His Word. Prayer and reading the Word of God will help you understand what God wants in your life and how to live a holy life. Always rely on the Holy Spirit to guide you into growing deeper in the understanding of God and His Word. As you do, you will begin to have more insight, a better spiritual life, and a more meaningful understanding of the Word.

The Bible is the answer to humanity's past, present, and future. It is filled with wisdom and divine instruction that will never, ever run dry. This spring, when you drink from it every day, will cause you to grow in Christ, and with faith, you will gain true joy by living the Christian life. Peace will come and you will have the happiness God has provided for us.

Love bears up under anything and everything that comes (1 Corinthians 13:7). Love always believes the best of every person. We have the wonderful Holy Spirit in us to remind us. He puts a check in us when we head in a wrong direction. The Holy Spirit will grow our faith and trust, will bring joy into our lives, and will help us grow as a Christian. Be sure you do not run out ahead of God. I know! I find myself doing this often in the flesh, doing my own thing! God gets my attention then, and I fall on my knees, praying. *"Help me God! Help my unbelief. Help me understand. Enlighten my mind about what you would have me do instead. Renew my spirit and my mind so I can do what is pleasing to you God, and that I will be created in righteousness and put on holiness. Let my mind be in you, which was in Christ Jesus! Amen."* This is the prayer I pray when I feel I am out of God's will. The peace of God *always* comes back to me, and I know He is there (the peace that passes all understanding).

Living in God's Grace

We do what we can to teach and learn the content of God's Word, but it is the Holy Spirit's job to awaken people to faith in Christ.

As Christians, we need to influence everyone we can to get in touch with scripture and to allow it to change every aspect of our lives as believers.

Christians need to live in ways that reflect His love and mercy. Culture today makes it hard to avoid distractions that are all around us. It is easy to get caught up in things that surround us. If we will immerse ourselves in scripture, then this will equip us, as temptations come, to stand strong. Our flesh is always prone to be pulled toward the enticement of this world. *Know this:* No amount of personal effort, good works, or religious deeds can earn a place for us in heaven! For it is by grace we are saved, through faith and not of ourselves. It is the gift of God, not of works.

God gave us the gift of eternal life through Jesus Christ our Lord (Ephesians 2:8).

No one can earn his way to heaven (Romans 6:29). A man is a sinner. All have sinned and come short of the glory of God (Romans 3:23).

Sin is transgressing God's Law. Sin includes lying, lust, cheating, evil thoughts, immoral behavior, deceit, and much more. Because of this, we cannot save ourselves. In spite of all of our sins, God is merciful. God is love. God is just.

God solved the problem of sin for all of us. God sent His only son, Jesus Christ, as His solution.

> In the beginning was the Word [Jesus] and the Word [Jesus] was God, and the Word [Jesus] was made flesh [born as a baby] and dwelt among us. (John 1:14)

He was hung on the cross and thereby paid the penalty for our sin. Then after three days, Jesus arose from the grave to purchase a place in heaven for all of us, if we will only accept Him. Jesus bore our sins in His body on the cross. And now He offers each one of us eternal life, heaven, as a free gift. Christ alone can give us eternal life. By trusting and resting upon Christ alone and what he has done for us, you can receive all that He has for you.

Believe on the Lord Jesus Christ and you will be saved (Acts 16:31). Remember, you can accept, trust, and believe in the Lord Jesus, who is the greatest person who ever lived. If you are praying to Him with a sincere desire to accept Him, Christ will come into your heart. Now give Him the driver's seat and let Him steer your life. Read His Word, the Bible, daily.

A Homeless Couple

For more than eight years now, my life has been up and down with sickness. During the hard times, I continue to trust God and know God's hand is present in my life. Doors have been opening daily as I pray and know that His Hand is on my home. After my husband, Daryl, passed in 2002, I opened my home to homeless people. Since then, others have lived with me on and off for years.

Recently, a couple came to live with me. They have been married twenty-five years. During that time, they have suffered several disasters. In 2012, while living in Joplin, Missouri, a devastating twister completely destroyed their home. More recently, in the autumn of 2017, floods in Texas again completely destroyed everything they had. This loving couple honors God and are a huge blessing to me and everyone in our home! Amanda and Lewis cook, clean, and watch over me like mother hens. They also drive me any where I need to go. It's wonderful to watch God working in such awesome ways every day. Much joy comes when you know God's hand is at work. This will bless you to your toes! We all worship God together in church. This makes my home—really, our home—stand strong because we are all believers with like faith.

"But whoso hath this world's goods and sees his brother has need and shutteth up his bowels of compassion for him, how dwelleth the love of God in him? My little children, let us not love in word, but in deed."

Our future *is* His Word. Isn't that amazing? And this is for as long as we live! The promises in the Bible are for *all* of us. Yes, every promise is ours! God moves every day in our lives and homes. He provides food, money, clothes, toothbrushes, shoes—literally anything this household needs! What a joy to see His provision day after day! Can you just imagine these daily blessings? Praise God! It should inspire your mind and fill your heart with joy and happiness! Every single day, every single thing this household needs, comes in. We are praying for a car to come in for Lewis and Amanda now, as she just returned to work as an RN. They want to get into a house of their own again. It is awesome to watch in absolute wonder as God's hand moves in their life! Being in God's will is the best thing we can do in life. It causes us to rejoice and to walk in and experience God's love daily.

Please pray with me for the people I invite into my home, that God will bless their path coming and going. Usually, they are homeless and have no one or nowhere else to go. Pray the Holy Spirit will draw souls to come to faith in Jesus Christ and grow in knowledge and truth through our Christian witness at all times! Thank you, Lord, thank you.

Heaven's Grocery Store

I was walking down life's highway a long time ago.
One day I saw a sign that read: Heaven's Grocery Store. As I got a little closer, the door opened wide. And when I came to myself, I was standing inside.
One handed me a basket and said, my child, shop with care.
Everything a Christian needed was in that grocery store.
And all you can't carry, you can come back tomorrow for more.
First, I got some Patience; Love was in the same row.
Further down was Understanding, I need that everywhere I go.
I got a box of Wisdom, a bag or two of Faith,
I just couldn't miss the Holy Ghost, for it was all over the place.
I stop to get some Strength and Courage to help me run this race.
I didn't forget salvation, for that was free.
So I tried to get enough of that to save you and me.
Then I started up to the counter, to pay my grocery bill,
For I thought I had everything to do my master's will.
As I went up the aisle, I saw Prayer and I just had to put that in.
For I knew when I stepped outside, I would run right into sin.
Peace and Joy were plentiful, they were on the last shelf.
Song and Praises were hanging near so I just helped myself.
Then I said to the angel, How much do I owe?
He just smiled and said, Just take them everywhere you go.
Again I smiled at him and said, How much do I owe?
He smiled again and said, my child, Jesus paid your bill a long time ago.

(Author unknown)

Holy Angels

Holy angels do not know what you think, but they do the righteous work that God has sent them to do as helpers, guardians, holy warriors, and messengers. The devil and fallen angels, called demons, bring lies and great evil, but they do not know what we think either.

Only God the Father, Jesus the Son (who is our Savior) and the Holy Spirit know what we think. Sometimes the word *trinity* is used to include all three together—God, Jesus, and the Holy Spirit. The Holy Spirit is sent to do the work of God the Father on the earth. Only God knows what is in the heart of man. In John 16:7–8, Jesus said,

> *Nevertheless I tell you the truth; it is expedient for you that I go away; for if I go not away, the Comforter will not come unto you; but if I depart, I will send him unto you. And when he is come, he will reprove the world of sin, and of righteousness and of judgment.*

This is the Holy Spirit that He will send to all that ask God to save them. He forgives all of our sins when we ask Him for forgiveness.

Atonement

If *the body of Christ, also called the church,* fully presented God's Word (*the whole council of God*), we would be making a *much greater impact* on the world. Today, God not only wants to forgive us of our sins, He also wants *all* to *know*: *He* loves us, desires to heal our bodies, will bless us, and will deliver us from discouragement and depression.

One of the main reasons the modern day church has been rendered so ineffective and irrelevant in many people's eyes is it is preached God is for the life hereafter. That makes having a relationship with the Lord a heaven and hell issue. It seems it isn't preached that *He loves us right here and now.* However, the church should present the Lord more accurately by saying: "*God will heal you and keep you healthy. He will deliver you from depression, despair, and strife the you find yourself in. God will prosper you in a way you could never accomplish through your effort alone*" (my words).

If we presented to others that God is not only for the forgiveness of sins, but for all of those other areas and more, they would see He truly is relevant to their daily lives! Christians need to speak the truth of the whole council of God. Healing should not be elevated above the forgiveness of sins, neither should healing be diminished below it.

Christ provided healing for us the same time He provided forgiveness of our sins. Healing isn't just an "add-on" nor an "added benefit" that happens sometimes. It is an essential part of what Christ came to do. God purchased healing for us just as He purchased forgiveness. It is all a part of His atonement. Some people believe healing is something only the Lord can do. They don't understand it is His will for us. I tell you, healing is a done deal and is available to you right now. Exactly the same as the forgiveness of sins. Here I am, mostly bedridden after being pronounced dead four times in my life. However, people prayed, believed, and I lived! I have also gotten stronger by prayer. Still, I wait for God to take me home to be with Him forever.

Healing is a blessing the Lord already purchased. God wants us well. Having faith and believing Him, based on His Word, healing is available for us to have. Biblical faith is believing in things it doesn't see. Jesus said to Thomas: *"Because thou hast seen Me, thou hast believed. Blessed are they that have not seen and yet have believed"* (John 20:29).

Faith gives substance to things that are not seen yet. Faith changes hope into reality. Faith will be there in the face of the evidence. Faith counts before seeing and has acted. You will see the substance and physical evidence manifests after you believe and act in faith first. There will be a reality then. And ye shall have them (the things you believe by faith). Faith counts the thing done before God has acted and sent answers. We cannot believe what the outward man tells us but must walk by the truth given in God's Word. God's Word instills faith in us and will teach us the difference in faith and hope. We will see the physical evidence of faith that is based upon the truth of the Bible.

The Word teaches us to function and hold onto our faith. The church needs to be properly taught on healing and salvation. Stay out of the man-ward side of faith and stay on the God-ward side of every battle in your mind. *Believe* is an action word. Hold tight to God's Word. Grasp on and hang on tight, and His Word will never fail you! Never! Never! The Word is God. It gives us hope when things are wrong all around us. It is His light for this dark world.

"Faith is the substance of things hoped for and the evidence of things not seen" (Hebrews 11:1).

Our hope is all in Him.

Hope

Our purpose in life is far greater than our personal fulfillment or peace of mind or even our happiness. We are born for God's purpose and by His design. Our ambition should be for the Him. The Lord, our Creator, is the owner and author of the manual containing His plans for our lives. Focusing on ourselves will never reveal nor fulfill the purpose for our lives. All hope is born out of God's promises to us. Jesus was, and still is, the master, illustrating God's truth with stories and parables revealing God's ways. By these, Jesus teaches us lessons on how to live right. Mankind's ways, which are evil and sinful, are different from God's ways which are far better, holy, and right. Praise is the elevator that takes us up out of despair. That is an example of one of God's ways.

Over the years, I've learned when God makes a promise, *He will fulfill it!* The Bible is full of his promises. God's Word is dependable and worthy of our trust. I've been going through a lot of pain in recent years. I found out really fast pain can destroy our trust in the Lord and our effective service of Him. Pain can render us bitter, sullen, unforgiving, angry, vengeful, and untrusting! All negative attitudes can kill any gain God could work in the midst of our pain. Thus, the enemy of our soul plans to use this thorn in our flesh.

In my case, pain—it could be something else for another person—was a weapon to defeat or impede God's continuing will and work in my life. Remember this: "all hope" is born from God and praise will elevate you up out of all negative things, including despair. The key to overcome the enemy of your soul and to have victorious living is to remember this: "*Love the Lord your God with all thine heart and with all thy soul and with all thy might."* Over the years, I've learned when God makes a promise, He will fulfill it. The Bible is full of His promises. God's Word is dependable. It is worthy of our trust. For me, there is no joy without Christ at the very center of all I do daily in my life. This my prayer for all who knows Christ.

Refresh and Grow

"*Those who refresh others will themselves be refreshed*" (Proverbs 11:2). God will empower us by his promise. Our faith teaches us there are no obstacles. Stumbling blocks are only stepping stones and is part of God's plan for our lives, that we might learn and be strong in our faith. Look at Peter! He was the only disciple to step out onto the water. The others stayed in the boat! His stepping stone was water, he believed! Then he looked at the wind and waves and he began to sink! He took his eyes off of Jesus! He doubted. "*We are human and doubt comes when we look at what is happening*" (Matthew 14:31). We get weak in faith. It is a much bigger deal when we as Christians do that. Remember His perspective. God can do all things. With Him, all things are possible God is with us when we are working for Him. The Bible tells us to be strong and of good courage. Do not be afraid nor be dismayed, for the Lord your God is with you wherever you go. We need to do our part and proclaim "the good news" for Him, and God will refresh the ones around us. Remember the Iraelites, they refused to enter Canaan because of the spies but Joshua said, "*Don't fear.*"

Joshua had faith, a strong belief. He believed all things to be possible. God gave him his enemies. God encouraged Joshua and he took his people to battle (Numbers 14:9). God will prepare us for all of our battles, whatever they maybe. He has called us for our struggles and to accept and enjoy in what He has called us to do. You will see his power moving in us, as we are the tools He will use, when we turn to Him for help. As we benefit from our faith, it will grow. We need not be concerned, for He alone is the power in everything.

A lot of times we unknowingly benefit from the seeds of faith we plant. Sometimes we never know if the planting goes to fruition or if it even continues after we plant the seed. Sometimes however, as in the following story, we do. We get to hear how the seed grew. How it was watered and prospered. And we are blessed!

I had been invited to a birthday party at a pizza place in town and knew most of the people that came. A few I did not know. As I was standing, looking around, a lady came up to me and said, "Do you remember me?"

"No, I don't," I replied.

She said, "My name is Mae," and she began to tell me a story that happened years ago! "Nan," she said, "about twenty years ago, you were shopping for a rug at the store I worked in at the time. I went over to see if I could help you. We started talking, and soon you began to pray with me! We were talking about God, and then you prophesied over me. One of the men I worked with saw this and later said to me, 'What was that crazy woman doing?'"

(God was already at work! The man was concerned if I was crazy or not. Yet, he was the one who delivered my rug a few days later! Of course I began to talk to him about Jesus. During our conversation, I asked if he'd ever read the Bible. He said, "No, I've never had a Bible." So Monday, off I went to our local Bible bookstore and bought a Bible. I then drove immediately to the furniture store and dropped it off to him. Surprisingly, he accepted it! I was so happy he took it that I rejoiced all the way home!)

Mae continued, "He found the sales slip you mistakenly left in the Bible. When he saw the receipt for $100.00, he said, 'I'm taking this back and getting the money for it!'"

Mae said she told him, "No, you can't. They won't give you money back for a Bible." Later, as he was getting ready to go home that evening, Mae said he had taken his sweatshirt off and wrapped it around the Bible, thinking no one would see it as he tucked it under his arm. However, Mae said she noticed the gold edges gleaming on the pages as he walked out the door! Mae told me he is a Christian now and still reading the Bible! I remembered telling him to start by reading Matthew, Mark, and John. What a joy sprung into my heart as she told me that story! My spirit needed refreshing, and I got it!

We never know how God will use things when we obey Him. Knowing God had used what I did brought much happiness and joy to my heart! I went home, rejoicing all the way and halfway on into the night! As I told others about the story, we were all blessed.

Be a blessing! Tell others about God and what he has done for you. The Bible also says to rebuke others of sin. Jesus rebuked religious materialism in the church and in the religious leaders of his day. Yes, you will find Christ, the living embodiment of love, rebuked sin when He saw it.

Prayers Can't Be Answered Unless They Are Prayed

Life without purpose is barren indeed,
There can't be a harvest unless you plant seed
There can't be attainment unless there's a goal,
and man's but a robot unless there's a soul.

If we send no ships out, no ships will come in,
and unless there's a contest, nobody can win.
For games can't be won unless they are played,
And prayers can't be answered unless they are prayed.

So whatever is wrong with your life today,
You'll find a solution if you kneel down and pray.
Not just for pleasure, enjoyment and health,
Not just for honors and prestige and wealth.

But pray for a purpose to make life worth living
And pray for the joy of unselfish giving.
For great is your gladness and rich your reward,
When you make your life's purpose the choice of the Lord.

(Author unknown)

A True Friendship

This is an addendum to what I previously have written. Recently God gave me a very prophetic dream, and I am compelled to include it.

I woke up from the dream and understood it was about the wisdom my friend, Shirley, has.

In the dream, King Solomon stood before the ark of the covenant of the Lord, offering up burnt and peace offerings for all of his servants, for he had many. As King Solomon was standing there, two women approached him. One's child had died, but both were claiming the living child to be theirs. As King Solomon listened to their stories, he made a decision. He said to his servants, "Bring me a sword." And they did and set it before the king. He said, "Divide the living child in two, and give half to one and half to the other."

The woman who was mother of this son was distraught and said, "O my lord, give her the living child, and in no wise slay it." But the other woman said, "Let it be neither mine nor thine, *but* divide *it*."

King Solomon knew immediately the first woman was the mother. He said not to slay the infant but give it to its rightful mother. All of Israel heard of the judgment and understood the wisdom of the king.

God told me that my friend, Shirley, has the wisdom of Solomon. I know that to be true as she has never spoken unwisely to me—never, in the over fifty years we have known each other. Every time I have needed truth, even when I didn't know I did, she has always, always, cut through everything and gave me wise counsel. She also gives all wisdom and glory to God, not of herself.

About the Author

Nan, mother of four, two boys and two girls, is also grandmother of four and great grandmother of two. Still residing in the Pacific Northwest, she has attended Bethany Pentecostal Church for fifty-three consecutive years.

Women's Teas at church is one of her favorite things to do. However, she does not do behind the scenes work or cooking anymore. Another of her favorite things to do (besides sharing the gospel) is lovingly share her Victorian decorated home with homeless women in need.

The picture of Nan was taken recently at one of the church teas.

www.ingramcontent.com/pod-product-compliance
Lightning Source LLC
Jackson TN
JSHW080957020225
78166JS00001B/37